Contents

METRIC SYSTEM

UNIT	ABBREVIATION		APPROXIMATE U.S. EQUIVALENT
Length			
		Number of Metres	
myriametre	mym	10,000	—————— 6.2 miles
kilometre	km	1000	0.62 mile
hectometre	hm	100	109.36 yards
dekametre	dam	10	32.81 feet
metre	m	1	39.37 inches
decimetre	dm	0.1	3.94 inches
centimetre	cm	0.01	0.39 inch
millimetre	mm	0.001	0.04 inch
Area			
		Number of Square Metres	
square kilometre	sq km *or* km²	1,000,000	0.3861 square miles
hectare	ha	10,000	2.47 acres
are	a	100	119.60 square yards
centare	ca	1	10.76 square feet
square centimetre	sq cm *or* cm²	0.0001	0.155 square inch
Volume			
		Number of Cubic Metres	
dekastere	das	10	13.10 cubic yards
stere	s	1	1.31 cubic yards
decistere	ds	0.10	3.53 cubic feet
cubic centimetre	cu cm *or* cm³ *also* cc	0.000001	0.061 cubic inch

Capacity				
		Number of Litres	Cubic	*Liquid*
kilolitre	kl	1000	1.31 cubic yards	
hectolitre	hl	100	3.53 cubic feet	
dekalitre	dal	10	0.35 cubic foot	2.64 gallons
litre	l	1	61.02 cubic inches	1.057 quarts
decilitre	dl	0.10	6.1 cubic inches	0.21 pint
centilitre	cl	0.01	0.6 cubic inch	0.338 fluidounce
millilitre	ml	0.001	0.06 cubic inch	0.27 fluidram

Mass and Weight			
		Number of Grams	
metric ton	MT *or* t	1,000,000	1.1 tons
quintal	q	100,000	220.46 pounds
kilogram	kg	1,000	2.2046 pounds
hectogram	hg	100	3.527 ounces
dekagram	dag	10	0.353 ounce
gram	g *or* gm	1	0.035 ounce
decigram	dg	0.10	1.543 grains
centigram	cg	0.01	0.154 grain
milligram	mg	0.001	0.015 grain

The College of West Anglia

Ramnoth Road • Wisbech •• PE13 2JE • Tel: (01945 582561)

Learning Resource Centre

The card holder is responsible for the return of this book
Fines will be charged on ALL late items

Sterling Publishing Co., Inc.   New York

To Woodworkers Everywhere

Edited by Timothy Nolan

Library of Congress Cataloging-in-Publication Data
Crabb, Tom.
  Band saw projects.

  Includes index.
  1. Woodwork. 2. Band saws. I. Title.
TT185.C77 1988   684'.083   88-2161
ISBN 0-8069-6718-8 (pbk.)

3 5 7 9 10 8 6 4

Copyright © 1988 by Tom Crabb
Published by Sterling Publishing Co., Inc.
Two Park Avenue, New York, N.Y. 10016
Distributed in Canada by Oak Tree Press Ltd.
℅ Canadian Manda Group, P.O. Box 920, Station U
Toronto, Ontario, Canada M8Z 5P9
Distributed in the United Kingdom by Blandford Press
Link House, West Street, Poole, Dorset BH15 1LL, England
Distributed in Australia by Capricorn Ltd.
P.O. Box 665, Lane Cove, NSW 2066
Manufactured in the United States of America

Sterling ISBN 0-8069-6718-8 Paper

Introduction

Woodworking is a fine old craft, at least as old as modern man himself. Evolution was probably speeded by the use of tools, and as man got smarter his tools got better (or possibly the other way around). So you might think there couldn't be anything new in woodworking—and you'd be right.

No new tools or techniques have been invented for hundreds of years, but things do change. Electricity, steel, and aluminum oxide all brought about change in the form of improvements rather than new inventions, and that isn't all bad.

The fun part of woodworking is making something you like or need to suit yourself, as well as understanding your tools, knowing what they will and won't do, and discovering your own ways of working the wood.

Every tool has its own character and area of expertise. It comes to you through a history of many small steps. Knowing the step isn't important, but knowing the tool as it stands before you is. This book gives you as much understanding of one tool, the band saw, as there is.

I hope that by the end of the book you can add another step to a fine old craft.

Using Your Saw

A LITTLE BACKGROUND

The band saw was first patented in England in 1808, and hasn't changed a great deal since then. Refinements have been made, but the basic concept, a steel band driven by two wheels is essentially the same.

A band saw is usually described by the diameter of its wheels, for example, a 14-inch band saw has wheels that are 14 inches in diameter. This measurement also relates directly to the *throat capacity* of the saw, a horizontal measurement from the blade to the frame at the table. This is usually a ¼ inch or so less than the diameter of the wheels. Another important measurement is the *depth capacity* (how far the upper guide can be raised), a reflection of the vertical distance between the wheels, usually one and a half times to twice their diameter.

Although housings may be shaped differently, set screws in different locations and castings heavier or lighter, most band saw parts are in the same place doing the same thing in the same way.

THE FRAME

The band saw frame holds all the parts. It should be strong, of course, so the wheels are not squeezed together when the blade is taut. (This rarely happens with two-wheel band saws but it can with the less rigid frames of the three-wheeled saws.) A good way to check your frame is to measure the distance between the upper and lower guides without a blade on the saw, then with a fully tensioned blade. They should be the same, and if they're not it could cause blade problems or excess vibration. To solve the problem, you should find a spot to add another brace which doesn't interfere with the operation of the saw, or use the saw with less than optimum blade tension.

MOTORS

A wide range of electric motors are used in band saws. The most common motor for the home shop band saw is a ½ to ¾ horse capacitor start motor. This size provides plenty of power without overburdening the utility company.

Whatever the size, the one essential requirement is that the motor run smoothly. If it doesn't, the blade will vibrate and cause the saw to walk across the floor whenever you try to use it. The best thing to do if your motor isn't running smooth is replace it, since the vibration usually indicates internal wear in the bearings.

WHEELS

A band saw's wheels must be round, balanced, aligned and have tires on them. If it sounds like a car's

Illus. 1. Hold a hardwood block against the tires to clean away wood chips.

wheels, it's because they have similar functions. The blade must ride on these wheels at about 35 miles per hour under about 12,000 p.s.i. (pounds per square inch). Fortunately, your band saw wheels are much easier to take care of than your car's.

Obviously, wheels must be round, because a lump will cause a dramatic change in blade tension which, in turn, will cause a vibration and a shorter blade life. Rounding the wheels is much easier than it sounds. To round the drive wheel clamp a guide or tool rest onto the band saw housing. Then take a plane blade or block of wood with sandpaper (about 80 grit is good) folded over the end and hold it against the tire at the crown (Illus. 1). Hold the block steady (don't push) until no more rubber comes off. This will take out any lumps there may be in the tire. Do the

same for the upper wheel. Either someone can turn the wheel for you or you can switch it with the drive wheel so the motor will do the work.

If sanding removes the tire crown then you need a new wheel, or at least a new tire. Re-tireing procedures can vary from band saw to band saw so it is best to check your saw's manual or with your dealer.

If you have a brand-new saw just out of the box, the tires will probably be a little lumpy, but ordinary use of the saw may be enough to round them out. The pressure on the tires from the blade should help work out some of the lumps. However, use the sanding block or plane blade after about an hour of use to make sure the tires are round.

You can clean the tires of chips and debris in the same manner, although for cleaning it's best to use just a block of hardwood with no sandpaper. This will remove only the chips and not the rubber.

BALANCE

Wheels are usually balanced at the factory, but if you experience a lot of vibration or have blade problems, it's a good idea to check them. Remove the blade and drive belt from the saw and give the drive wheel a little spin, enough for a revolution or two. When it stops, put a pencil mark at the bottom of the wheel and spin it again. If the pencil mark stops at the bottom again, there is a heavy spot in the wheel. Spin the wheel a few more times and if the pencil mark is always at the bottom, then add a little weight at the top of the wheel (Illus. 2). Put either soldering wire or a piece of metal inside the rim of the wheel, opposite the heavy spot. (Epoxy works best for this.) If you have a very accurate scale, then the added weight can be weighed and holes drilled in the wheel at the pencil mark. Just

make sure the drill fillings match the weight that was added. The added or subtracted weight should be evenly spaced on both sides of the spot being corrected.

ALIGNMENT

Band saw wheels must run vertically one over the other. This is a fact of life. Band saws, as they come from the factory, usually have the wheels aligned, but it's a good idea to check the alignment before you use the saw. Wheels can get out of alignment from use or vibration.

On most saws the top wheel is fixed in position with retainer rings while the bottom wheel is adjustable. To get the bottom wheel directly under the top wheel hold a straightedge against the edge of the wheels (Illus. 3). Align the wheels by moving the lower wheel in or out on the shaft until they are exactly vertical. Secure the wheel in place with the set screw.

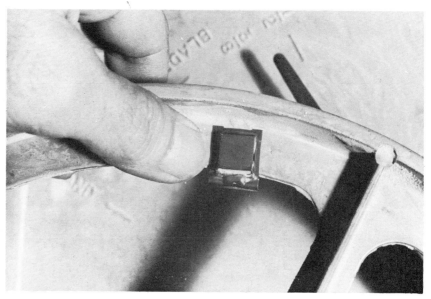

Illus. 2. A factory-added wheel weight to balance the wheel.

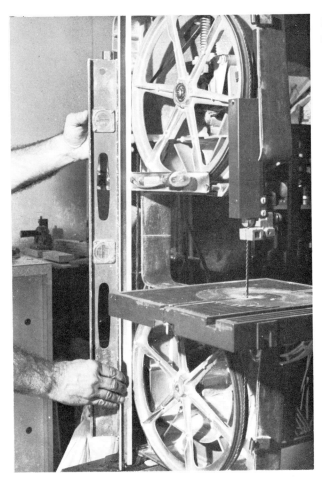

Illus. 3. Aligning the wheels with a straight-edge and level.

Illus. 4. Square up from the table to check alignment.

Illus. 5. Adjust the tracking by turning the screw slot in the center of the shaft. The tension spring (top) may weaken over the years. Add a washer to make up for lost tensioning power.

It's a good idea to check the alignment from time to time as well as the tightness of the set screw on the bottom wheel (Illus. 4).

TRACKING

Band saw blades should run in the middle of the wheels right on top of the tire crown. *Tracking* is adjusting the position of the blade on the wheel. This is done by tilting the upper wheel backwards or forward. The upper wheel is mounted on a shaft with a hinge so it can be tilted to either side of vertical by simply turning a screw (Illus. 5). Some saws have the screw threaded through the shaft so it pushes on the saw's housing, while others are threaded through the housing and push against the shaft. Either way they do the job without fuss.

Adjust the tracking if you're fine-tuning only. Don't adjust it if you have a serious tracking problem. This usually indicates misaligned or worn parts on the saw.

Putting a new blade on the saw is a different story. Once you've gotten the blade around the wheels, take up about half of the working tension and move all the guides away; then turn the lower wheel by hand and the blade should find its position on the wheel (if it strays off the crown you may have to adjust it). Restore the full tension and, standing to one side of the saw, flick it on and off. When it slows down give the new blade one last check; then replace the front cover, bearings, and guides. Turn on the saw and watch the blade. It should stay in the same position in relation to the guides.

GUIDES

The band saw has two sets of guides: one above the table and one below it. They support the blade above and below the stock and prevent the blade from wandering in directions of its own choosing. Each has two side-to-side guides and a rear thrust bearing.

The guides on either side of the blade give the blade support from side to side. On most home-shop band saws these are metal squares about ⅜ inch square held in a housing by a set screw. The housing adjusts back and forth to allow for different widths of blades.

Position the guides just behind the gully of the teeth and set them to the blade so they touch without pressure. Set the guides after the blade tension and tracking are adjusted. Don't force the blade to one side or the other when setting the side-to-side guides.

While these guides are usually metal, some woodworkers prefer to use wooden guides, either lignum vitae or teak. If you use wooden blocks, squeeze them against the blade and run the saw for a minute before using. This lets the blade "wear in" and the natural oils in the wood lubricate the blade.

A blade thrust bearing acts as a guide by supporting the blade from behind. This bearing keeps the blade from being pushed off the crown of the tires when you run a piece of wood through. It also keeps the blade tracking in place. Make sure the bearing spins freely and is adjusted so the blade does not quite touch it when you are not sawing.

The upper guides are on an arm which moves up and down to adjust for different thicknesses of wood (Illus. 6). This guide should just clear the top of the stock when sawing, and the arm should be square with the table. When you raise and lower the arm, it may not stay the same dis-

Illus. 6. A typical upper blade guide arrangement.

tance from the blade. When this happens, shim the arm or the plate which holds it to the saw housing.

VIBRATION

Anything that goes around and around very fast is prone to vibration, and when you are doing fine and intricate work this can be most annoying. If your band saw is vibrating and none of the previous steps cure it, check the table or bench under the saw. Sometimes the table legs will flex with any irregularity in the motion of the saw. It's a good idea to add diagonal supports to your band saw table whether it vibrates or not.

Cutting Up

BLADES

Band saw blades come in different widths, thicknesses, number of teeth per inch, etc. I often wish there was just one perfect blade for every job, but no such luck.

The blade's width (the length from the front of the teeth to the back of the blade) directly relates to the diameter of a curve it will cut and the amount of tension it will take. The shorter the width, the sharper the curve it will cut (Illus. 7). Blade widths start at 1/16 inch and go up, although a 1/16-inch blade is not one of my favorites. I find it too delicate—not able to take enough tension and in need of a lot of tracking adjustment. It's really a specialty blade, and you should only use it when nothing else will do.

The 1/8-inch blade is also a specialty blade for cutting tight corners (1/4-inch radius) but because it can take more tension it's a lot less inclined to bow when cutting. You can get 1/8-inch blades with different number of teeth per inch, depending on how thick the wood you're cutting is.

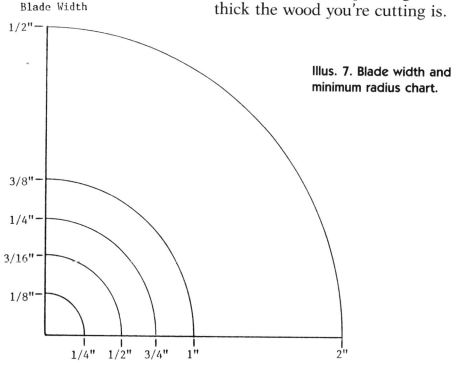

Illus. 7. Blade width and minimum radius chart.

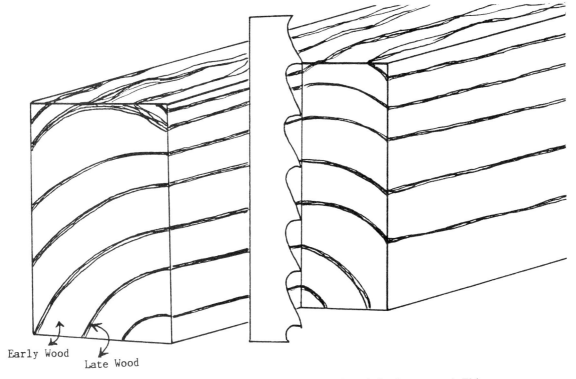

Early Wood

Late Wood

Illus. 8. Some grains have two thicknesses: the early wood and the late wood. This can produce some unpleasant sawing results.

The all-around standard (and my favorite) blade is the ¼ inch. It comes in a large variety of teeth patterns, number of teeth per inch, types of metal and different thicknesses. All of these options let you match the blade to the job that needs to be done and still cut a ¾-inch radius. The number of teeth range from 4 to 15 per inch, patterns are available from hook to skip to hack saw, and the blade will take a lot of tension and a fast feed rate.

Blades from ⅜ to ¾ inch, which are the most common for non-industrial band saws, are essentially the same as the ¼ inch, except they can take more stress. The home saw, however, will not tension a wider blade

properly so the advantage is somewhat negated. The standard wisdom (that a wider blade will saw straighter) is true if you are sawing a straight line freehand, but, with a rip fence, a sharp blade and proper tension, the ¼-inch blade will saw just as straight as a ¾-inch blade. The one advantage you can get in a wider blade is less teeth per inch, which may help when sawing thick or resinous wood.

The number and shape of the teeth on the blade are also important. One rule of thumb is to always have at least three teeth in the wood. Anything less and you can't hold the wood to the saw table or feed the saw fast enough and still keep control.

This is why we have 15 teeth per inch blades, and the thinner the wood, the more teeth you should use.

Most any blade will cut with efficiency across the grain as long as there are three teeth in the wood. But when it comes to sawing a raw log (resawing) or cutting with the grain (ripping), the story changes. Some grains have two different thicknesses: the early wood, which is the first growth of the spring, is less dense and lighter in color; the second growth period comes in middle to late summer and produces harder and more dense wood (Illus. 8). This change in density has an unpleasant effect on sawing, especially resawing, because as the blade passes from the softer to the harder grain it deflects to one side or the other (Illus. 9). (This is one cause for the little up and down ripples across the face of the wood after resawing.) A properly tensioned and sharp blade can reduce this, but it's also a case of the right blade for the job.

A skip tooth blade starts cutting as soon as the teeth contact the wood. This pushes the wood back away from the tooth, so the blade doesn't hold the wood. On the other hand, the hook-tooth blade first grabs the wood with its hook, pulling the wood to it, then begins to cut (Illus. 10). This keeps the blade from deflecting since it has a grip. It also speeds the feed rate and reduces the amount of pressure needed.

Band saw blades have the most an-

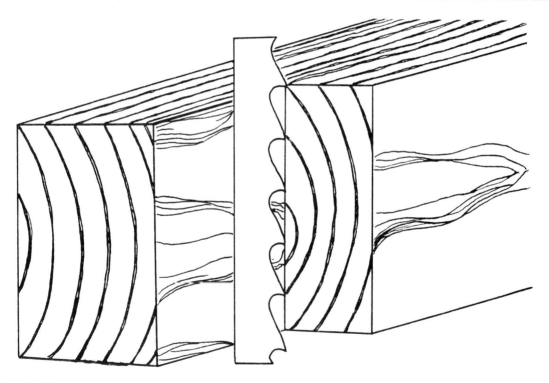

Illus. 9. When resawing, the saw blade can be deflected by the greater density of the wood. Use a slower feed rate to avoid this.

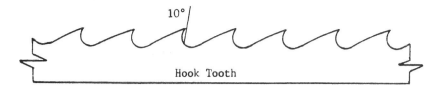

Illus. 10a. The hook tooth blade has a 10° rake angle which pulls the wood to it.

noying habit of bowing (or bending) in the cut. This can be due to the fence not being parallel to the blade, but a more common cause is excess feed pressure which is probably the result of the blade getting dull and the user getting impatient. The pressure applied to the front of the blade is transferred to the back as tension or a stretching effect. This, in turn, causes a compression of the front so the blade begins to bow. Once the bowing begins there is nothing you can do but stop the saw, back the wood out, change blades and start again.

Gullies in the band saw blade are the spaces between the teeth. Their size and shape can affect the efficiency of the blade. For example, if there weren't any gullies there would be only one tooth. Not a good design for wood.

As the teeth chisel their way through the wood they pull chips into the gullies. The chips usually stay in the gullies until the tooth clears the wood; then they fall out. The larger the gully, the more wood it can hold. Thus, sawing through a thick piece of wood with a 15 tooth blade with clogged gullies creates a lot of friction. The 4 and 6 teeth hook-tooth pattern has a deep, rounded gully which holds a lot of chips and tends not to clog when sawing dried wood of any thickness. A skip-tooth blade uses a different tack. The gullies are not so deep but every third or fifth tooth, depending on the number of teeth, has no *set*—the tooth doesn't lean to one side or the other but stands straight forward. This tooth doesn't cut the wood as such but slides through the kerf, cleaning out the debris. Personally, I favor this design when sawing green or sappy wood.

Used to be when the only blade you could buy was made from carbon steel. Today, although it's still the most widely used blade, bimetal ones are available as well. While I still use carbon steel blades for some work (especially the narrower blades like the

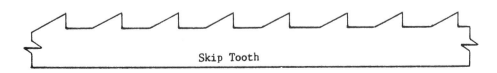

Illus. 10b. The skip-tooth blade is more mild-mannered, with a smoother cut for ripping or resawing.

⅛ inch) for most of my sawing I use a bimetal blade.

The blades have two big differences. The first is the price, while the bimetal blade may cost two to three times more than the carbon steel one, it'll last ten to twenty times longer. This leads to the second difference—the bimetal blade takes heat better. Carbon steel is tempered to increase its hardness but it'll start to lose its temper, or anneal, at about 400°F. This'll make the blade brittle and chippy. Bimetal blades, on the other hand, can take 1200°F. before annealing begins. This is because teeth of the bimetal blade are cobalt steel, which is much more heat tolerant than carbon steel.

Most of us can't work with tension, but a band saw blade can't work without it. (Band saw blades are a lot tougher than we think.) Tension for a ¼-inch blade on an industrial band saw is about 30,000 p.s.i., about half of that for a home shop saw (which, on the whole isn't too bad). But that's just for a ¼-inch blade. The prospects of tensioning a ½- or ¾-inch blade on a home saw are out of the question. I usually tension a ¼-inch blade to the ½-inch mark on the tension scale, which is around 12,000 p.s.i. on my band saw, and double the tension on every blade I use: a ⅟₁₆ is tensioned to ⅛, a ⅛ goes to a little over the ¼ mark, and so on.

The standard thickness of carbon and bimetal blades is between .020 and .025 of an inch. Thinner blades are available in thickness of .014 to .018, primarily for three-wheeled band saws. Since here the blade must turn an extra corner to go around the third wheel, blade life tends to be shorter. This is compensated for by making the blade thinner so it turns the corners more easily. Since the three-wheeled band saw frame cannot match the blade tension of the two wheeler frame, the blade can be thinner without giving up much.

The mechanism that creates the tension is a spring which rides up and down on a threaded rod and raises the upper wheel, thus stretching the blade. Most band saws use this mechanism, which works quite well until the spring fatigues. Then your tension indicator will read the proper tension but the blade won't have it. When this happens, measure the spring in your saw against a new spring. If they're the same, fine, but if one is shorter add a washer or two to the top of the spring to make up the difference. Even just a ⅛ inch can make a noticeable difference in the blade tension. Another way to increase tension is to have your band saw blades made an inch shorter.

Finally, there is the blade's speed of travel, expressed in surface feet per minute (sfm). Most band saws from the factory run at about 3,000 sfm (why, I'm not sure), which is over 34 miles an hour. This is a little fast for my taste. I used that speed for years before it occurred to me that I could slow it down and gain more control plus a little more torque from the motor. All you have to do is change the pulleys.

The band saw I use now came from

the store turning 2,800 sfm, and once I got it set up I started figuring out a way to slow it down to about 1,800 sfm (about 20 mph), my favorite speed. The saw was equipped with a 2½-inch pulley on the motor and a 5-inch pulley on the drive wheel, and a change to a 2-inch pulley on the motor and a 6-inch pulley on the saw gave me a speed of 1,831 sfm. Close enough.

The formula I used was

$$\left(\frac{R\ P1}{P2}\right) 3.14D = \text{inches per minute.}$$

This is divided by 12 to get feet per minute. Multiply "R", the RPM's of the motor by "P1", the diameter of the motor pulley, then divide by "P2", the diameter of the band saw pulley. Multiply this number by 3.14, then by "D", the diameter of the band saw wheel which drives the blade. Your result will be in inches per minute, which is then divided by 12 to get feet per minute.

By shifting "P1" and "P2" (the diameters of the pulleys) up and down you can find the speed which suits you the best. After using the saw a little while you should find a speed you prefer, but if you are new with your saw don't be in any hurry. You'll catch on soon enough.

Another benefit of a slower blade speed is that each tooth has more time to cool before its next turn in the wood, which will help the blade last longer. That's something we'd all like to do.

FOLDING THE BLADE

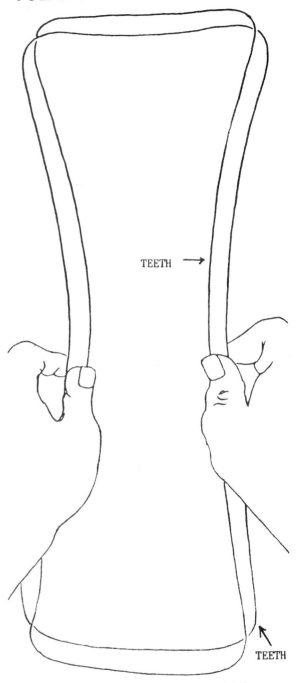

TEETH →

TEETH

Illus. 11. If the party gets dull, try folding a band saw blade to liven things up. The teeth should face in and the top and bottom should fold away from you. A little help from your knee may be needed.

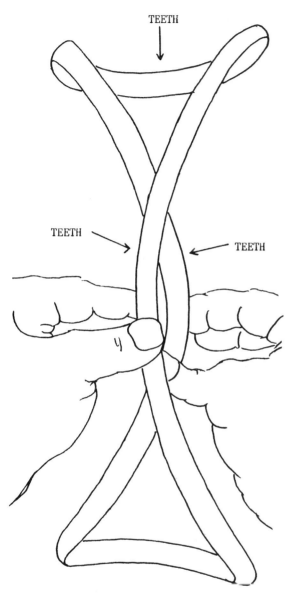

TEETH

TEETH

TEETH

Illus. 12. At this point you must switch hands. This is where control is sometimes lost.

The mark of a real band saw owner is knowing how to fold a band saw blade. This has nothing to do with your ability to use the tool, it just means that you had enough time on your hands one day to figure out how to make one large circle fold into three small ones.

The very best way to learn folding is to watch someone else do it, then try it until you get it right. There is no next best way. Short of this, instructions have been written, photographs taken and drawings drawn but in the end it's just do it until you get it right.

Start by holding the blade in front of you, with the teeth pointing in. As you bring the sides of the blade together in the middle turn the teeth so that they are facing each other (Illus. 11). Two circles should form above and below your hands and begin to fold away from you. (They will not do this willingly; some help from your knee may get it started.)

When you bring the two sides of the blade together, the top and bottom circles should face each other and be almost 90° from you. Cross the blade by switching the right side to the left hand and the left to the right hand (Illus. 12). (This is where control is sometimes lost.) The blade should now cross above and below your hands, and, as you widen the middle circle, the top and bottom circles should get smaller until all the circles are about the same size (Illus. 13). As you widen the middle circle, the top and bottom ones should be folding into your hands, and at some point the blade collapses into three circles

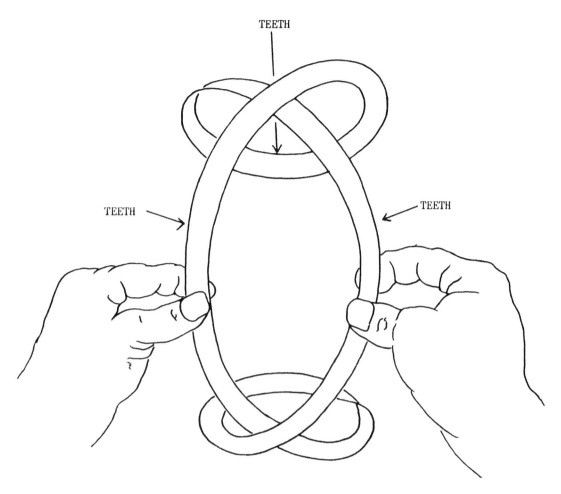

TEETH

TEETH

TEETH

Illus. 13. As you widen the space between your hands, the top and bottom circles curl into the center, overlapping each other.

all the same size. This is what we're after.

Many of us suffer from the delusion that if we have done it once we can do it again. Well, if you've done it once you'd better do it again, right away. I think about five times in a row ought to do it.

Keep in mind that the explanation is done in sequence while the actual act takes place all at once. The blade is twisted and brought together, the top and bottom circles begin to fold out, all at the same time. Then the next thing you know, the whole thing is over. It's a miracle.

A blade is hard to store and is subject to damage if it's stored unfolded and just hung on the wall, or stuffed behind a cabinet. The best idea is to fold them and put them back in the box they came in for storage. Also, since it seems like a physical impossibility it can be fun at parties.

RESAWING

I don't know anyone with a band saw who hasn't, from time to time, come across a nice chunk of wood in log form and wanted to saw it into lumber for some special project. Band saws do this kind of work very well, thus giving you access to woods which are not commercially available. Say when someone admires one of your projects and asks what kind of wood you used, you can tell them proudly, "Fungus stained elm crotch."

Before taking log to band saw, however, you should have one side flat to lay on the saw table. If the wood is a species that splits well I usually split off a side and plane it flat with an electric hand plane. If it doesn't split or is more than two feet long I usually saw off a flat side with a chain saw.

Lay the flat side on the workbench, and with a square draw a vertical line up both ends of the log as wide as the board you want. It's usually best to tack a wooden straightedge between the lines, so you have something to saw along, since it's a rare log that is perfectly round (Illus. 14). This should get you two flat sides 90° from each other, one for the saw table and the other for the rip fence. Once this is done then the rest of the sawing can be done with accuracy.

It is usually helpful when resawing to put a wedge in the kerf behind the blade. This keeps the blade from being pinched and lets the chips fall where they may.

Illus. 14. Use a wooden straightedge when resawing a log into usable stock.

Joints, Jigs, Scales & Sticky Stuff

JOINTS

Fancy joints didn't used to be fancy for fancy's sake, they were necessary for a strong connection between two pieces of wood. We can now do that with glue, so fancy joints are now just that. We don't need dovetails or keyed joints except to show off (and there's nothing wrong with that.) But understanding why you do something is the beginning of doing it well. Remember, a joint needs to be two things: as strong as needed and as attractive as wanted. Most basic joints can be cut on the band saw.

One of my favorite joints is the rabbet (Illus. 15a), from the Old French, rabattre, meaning to beat down, not the animal from which glue can be made. Beating is not a recommended way to make a joint, but you'll see the connection.

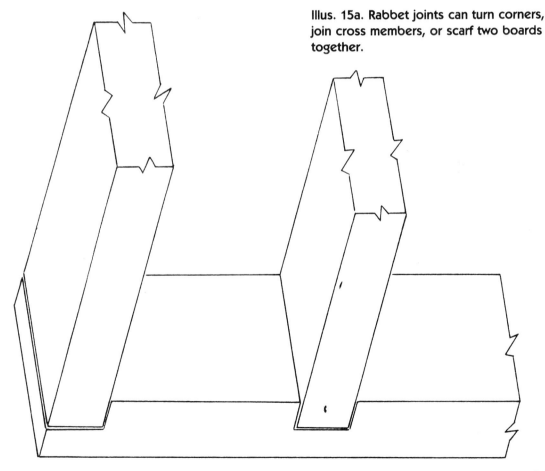

Illus. 15a. Rabbet joints can turn corners, join cross members, or scarf two boards together.

The rabbet joint can form a corner, connect a crosspiece in the middle of another board, or connect boards end to end. It doubles the gluing surface and therefore is quite a strong but simple joint, and because the band saw can be easily jigged (I'll get to that shortly) it can cut the joint accurately.

Adding a finger not only makes the rabbet fancier but much stronger because it increases the gluing surface by about a third (Illus. 15b). The joint now has a built-in lock. Dovetailing the finger won't make it any stronger but will add intrigue (Illus. 15c).

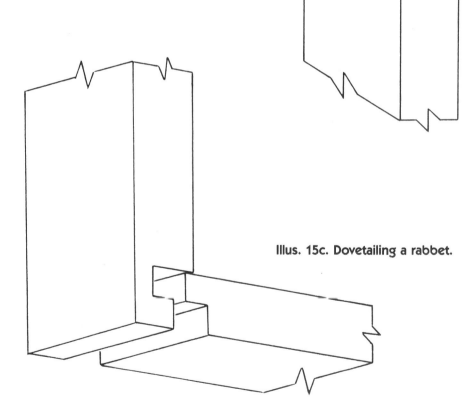

Illus. 15b. Adding a finger can make a sort of second rabbet.

Illus. 15c. Dovetailing a rabbet.

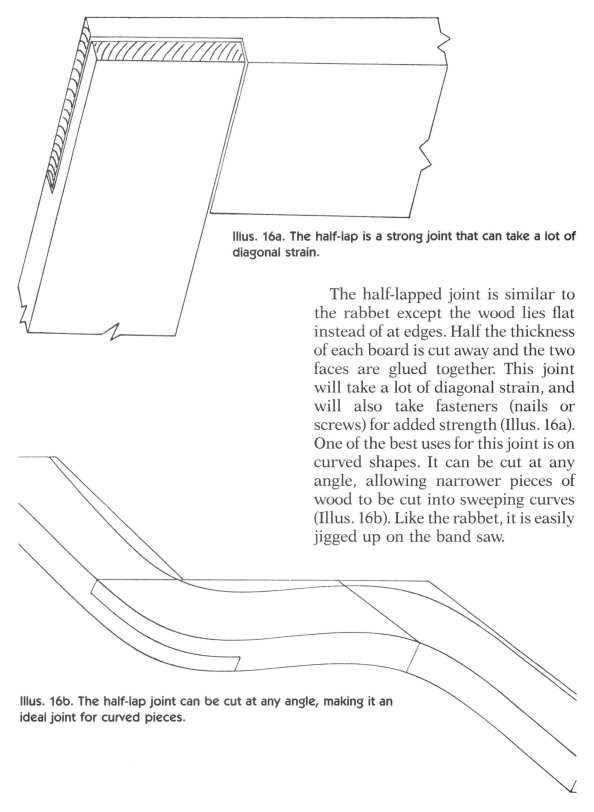

Illus. 16a. The half-lap is a strong joint that can take a lot of diagonal strain.

The half-lapped joint is similar to the rabbet except the wood lies flat instead of at edges. Half the thickness of each board is cut away and the two faces are glued together. This joint will take a lot of diagonal strain, and will also take fasteners (nails or screws) for added strength (Illus. 16a). One of the best uses for this joint is on curved shapes. It can be cut at any angle, allowing narrower pieces of wood to be cut into sweeping curves (Illus. 16b). Like the rabbet, it is easily jigged up on the band saw.

Illus. 16b. The half-lap joint can be cut at any angle, making it an ideal joint for curved pieces.

The saddle joint is a slightly more complicated version of the half-lap, because the workpiece is laid out in thirds instead of halves (Illus. 17). If you want something a little stronger than the half-lap this is a good joint to use. It's stronger than the half-lap because it has twice the gluing surface. It's more complicated to cut but it can still be jigged and sawn out quickly and accurately.

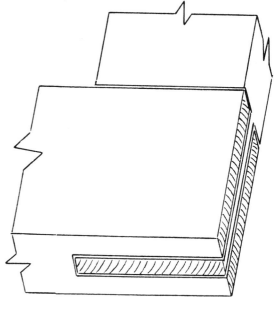

Illus. 17. The saddle joint is a more complicated version of the half-lap.

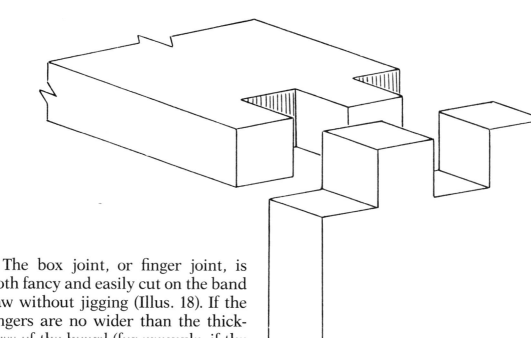

The box joint, or finger joint, is both fancy and easily cut on the band saw without jigging (Illus. 18). If the fingers are no wider than the thickness of the board (for example, if the board is ¾ inch then the fingers should be ¾ inch or less in height) and if there are more than two fingers then this joint looks great. If the board is too narrow for this, then another joint (such as the rabbet or mitre) is called for.

Illus. 18. The box, or finger, joint is strong and fancy.

The bird's mouth joint (so-called because it looks like an open bird's mouth) is good for scarfing pieces together end to end (Illus. 19a). It results in a matching scissors effect which resists edge and side loading better than most scarf joints. You can even use it to join curved pieces by cutting the joint from an "X" pattern at a 45° angle (Illus. 19b).

To cut an angle on the band saw, mark the angle in the edge of a board (or even your bench top) with a protractor, then pick up the angle with a bevel gauge and set it on the band saw. This is the only way to accurately set and cut an angle on the band saw.

If the joint is going to take a heavy load, it's a good idea to use dowel pins (as shown in Illus. 19a). If one side of the joint is not visible in the finished product then screws can also be used. However, with the added gluing surface and efficiency of most joints, you shouldn't need dowel pins or screws.

Illus. 19a. The bird's-mouth scarf joint is easy to cut on the band saw when jigged up.

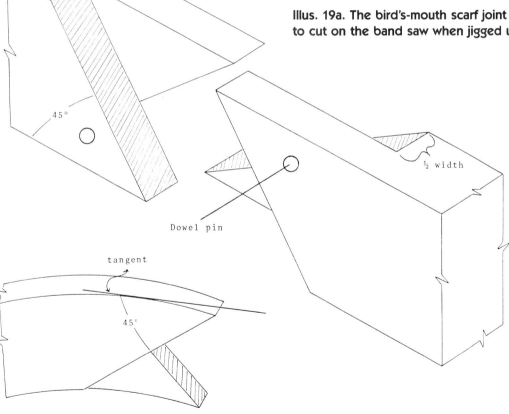

45°

½ width

Dowel pin

tangent

45°

Illus. 19b. Laying out the bird's-mouth scarf at 45° from a tangent for joining curved pieces.

JIGS

Generally, jigs make your life a little easier. Specifically, they help you make two or more exact cuts faster and with more accuracy. Some jigs are more complicated than the piece they make, but the simpler the jig, the better, so it's usually best not to use these. Jigs must be made with care and accuracy because whatever mistake is built into the jig will be reproduced in the work every time it's used.

Some jigs have become so integrated and essential to woodworking that we don't think of them as jigs at all. A rip fence (Illus. 20) is a perfect example: a jig for cutting a straight line. How ingenious. You can add stops to the rip fence for consistent cuts, hold-downs and hold-ins for special situations, and an auxiliary fence for tapers and curves.

The mitre fence, or cross-cut fence, is another jig we take for granted, but it can also be "re-jigged" with stops and hold-downs to expand its use (Illus. 21–22). With the band saw an auxiliary fence, as wide as the saw table, is usually added (Illus. 23). This allows you to clamp the workpiece to the fence or hold both ends on either side of the blade. Cut a rabbet ¼ inch or so into the fence so that the blade clears the work piece without cutting into the fence.

A circle-cutting jig can speed things along when cutting circles for wheels or other projects (Illus. 24–25). Basically, it's a long blade guide with a trammel point attached, under which the center of the circle pivots.

Illus. 20. Squaring a rip fence from the saw table at both ends.

Illus. 21. Using both hands on the mitre fence helps keep the stock in position.

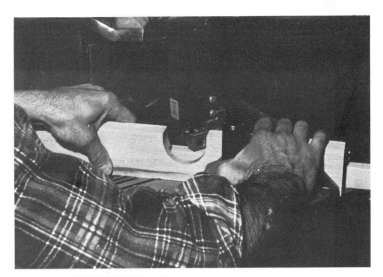

Illus. 22. Adding stops to the mitre fence, one for the depth of the cut and the other for the position of the cut.

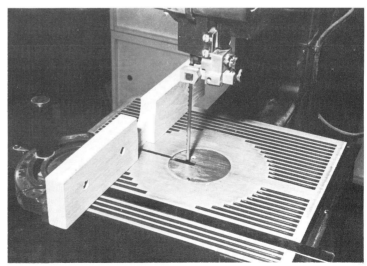

Illus. 23. A typical auxiliary fence added to the mitre fence.

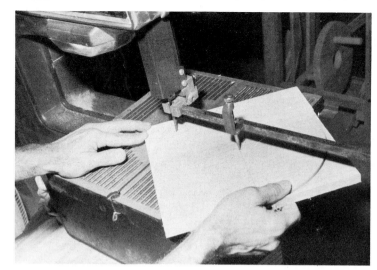

Illus. 24. The circle-cutting jig replaces the blade guide and uses a trammel point to hold the center of the circle in place.

Illus. 25. The circle-cutting jig must be squared from the teeth of the blade to the center of the circle.

The blade guides on my band saw are ⅜-inch square, so I replaced the right blade guide with a ⅜-inch square steel rod 16 inches long. If you do this, place the trammel point at the radius of the circle (measured from the blade). You must square the trammel point from the blade's teeth, otherwise the circle you saw won't be what you wanted.

Jigging up for a special joint can sometimes be more fun than actually cutting the joint. The bird's mouth is a good example (Illus. 26). For years I cut this joint by hand while the band saw sat idly by. Then, one day, it occurred to me that I could cut this joint on the band saw if the pieces were shorter than five feet.

Begin by making one cut at a time in a scrap piece of wood and then seeing what needs to be done next. Make the first cut with the saw table at 45° (see page 25) with a stop on the cross-cut fence and the table. Saw the wood halfway through, then turn it

28

Illus. 26. The bird's-mouth scarf joint can be cut on the band saw by first sawing the 45° "X" using the saw table at 45° and the mitre fence with stops.

over and make the same cut on the other side. This results in a 45° "X" with half of the "X" on opposite sides of the material.

The second saw cut requires a jig to hold the corner of the workpiece at 45° to the level saw table (Illus. 27). This jig is a piece of scrap the same width as the 45° stock cross-cut. This piece has a fence on one side and a vertical piece on the other where the workpiece can be clamped. Attach another 45° piece, half the width of

the material, to the fence so the work won't slide forward. The whole thing will slide along the saw's rip fence with the upper guides functioning as a stop.

This affair works pretty well; however, if the workpiece is very long, it helps to have a support behind you to help hold up the other end. I've found the easiest support to use is another person since they adjust easily, otherwise you can use a step ladder.

Jigs can be quite personal—what

Illus. 27. Make the second cut on the bird's-mouth with a jig which will hold the material at 45° from the table and slide along the rip fence.

works for one person may not work for another (Illus. 28). Any jig you haven't used before should be tested before you saw into your walnut. You may not like the jig, or may want to add or subtract to suit yourself.

Illus. 28a. This jig for cutting like corners may require some rehearsal time.

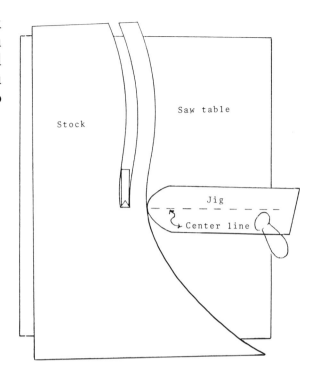

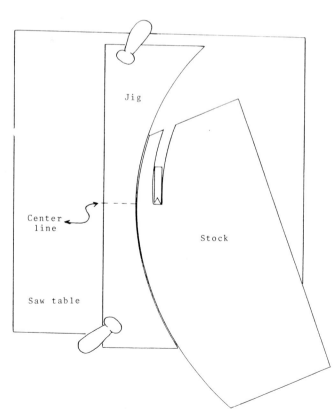

Illus. 28b. This jig is easy to use for sawing symmetrical curves.

STICKY STUFF

In the old days gluing wood was simple: you filled the joint with hide glue, put it together, then added a few nails or screws to make sure. Since the 1940's, however, glues have gotten more sophisticated. As industrial products filtered down to the home craftsman, choices of sticky stuff have increased threefold. The problem now is—which glue for which project? Decisions, decisions.

Basically, there are three types, all stronger than the wood itself. The first consists of polyvinyl resin emulsions (white or milky stuff) and a close cousin, polyvinyl acetate, or PVA (yellow or brown stuff), also known as Tite-Bond and Elmer's Carpenter's Glue. Then there are the epoxies, especially the five-minute kind, and finally the ever-popular, but lately much maligned, urea-formaldehyde glue, also known as Weldwood Plastic resin. Each does its job very well, but each has its particular specialty.

Urea-formaldehyde adhesives have been around since the 1930's and are still widely used in industry today. It has some properties which are quite useful and some which are a nuisance. One nuisance is that it must be mixed with water to the consistency of cream, then applied without dripping it all over the shop. Another is that, after the glue has set, it is hard and brittle, which is both good and bad. It sands well, but it will take the edge off a cutting tool in quick fashion. This glue also takes a long time

to cure (or dry), especially in wintertime (a little heat from a light bulb can help speed things along—but don't rush). The excess must be hard before unclamping.

Finally, there's the formaldehyde. Some people show a sensitivity to the fumes and others to getting it on their skin—on the other hand, some of us have no sensitivity at all. Several years ago it was reported that formaldehyde was a carcinogen, but the American Environmental Protection Agency has made no move to remove urea-formaldehyde glues from the shelves, so the cautions on the can should be followed to the letter.

Urea-formaldehyde's good side is that it will stick any kind of wood to any kind of wood. The glue squeezes out of joints with ease, leaving a thin and almost invisible glue line. The cured glue is hard, machines well, resists moisture and high temperature better than PVAs, and does not creep (more on that later). Brushes and mixing tools can be cleaned in soap and water before the glue sets up.

Epoxy has taken some time to reach the workshop since its development in the 1940's. The catalysts and resin must be mixed quite accurately just before use in order to achieve the best results. Different formulas require different catalysts to resin ratios; 7 to 1, 5 to 1 and lately 1 to 1 ratios are common. Epoxy does tend to be a little on the stiff side and does not squeeze out well, so the glue line is almost always visible. Quantities larger than held in the small tubes or syringe are not always easy to find (your best bet is a marine hardware store), and formulas can vary widely. So, while you may not be able to get one brand to work well another may be just the ticket.

However, epoxy has several things going for it. It's a great gap filler, requires only contact to achieve a good bond and when cured it is hard and machinable. Epoxy is the best adhesive to use for outdoor application because of its great resistance to moisture and temperature changes. Mix it with a little sawdust and it'll make a very good filler. It is always darker than the wood, so it won't hide anything, and is so strong it'll be there forever.

Thermosetting polyvinyl emulsions, the brown or yellow PVA's, have certainly found a place in my heart. You can use them right out of the bottle, they grab quickly, and they don't seem to irritate anybody. The stuff squeezes out of joints well, leaving a thin glue line, and it never gets too hard. This lets a joint come and go naturally without breaking, and also won't take the edge off your cutting tools.

However, you can't use PVA's outdoors, because it has little resistance to moisture and it tends to weaken and stretch as the temperature goes up. The glue may not get too hard, but that also makes it difficult to sand without clogging the sandpaper. The main limitation of PVA's, however, is called cold creep or cold flow. Cold creep is the tendency for the glue to yield to stress along the glue line, thus it lacks resistance to continuously applied loads, such as would be found in wood bending.

Keeping three different kinds of glue around the shop is the best bet, and not too much to ask.

SCALING UP

Enlarging patterns, or scaling up, is one of those things you have to do sometimes before you can get to the real fun, like sweeping the workshop or changing blades. There are at least three methods you can use: the grid method, the pantograph, and my favorite, the copy machine.

The grid method is probably the oldest, slowest and least accurate, but sometimes it's the only method that will work. The idea is to lay out a grid the size you need and then make a short mark every time a line on the original pattern crosses a line of a square. After you marked all the intersections, all that's left is filling in the lines (Illus. 29).

Part of the difficulty of this method is drawing all those little squares, but you don't have to do that every time. Take a piece of white poster board, about 11 by 14 inches, and draw appropriate-sized squares with a black ballpoint or soft-tip pen. When you want to scale up a drawing, lay a sheet of paper over the poster board and tape it down at the corners. You can see the little squares right through most papers. When finished,

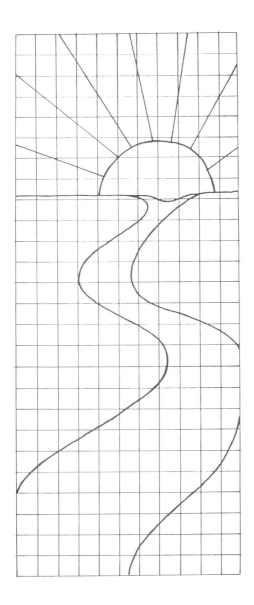

Illus. 29. An example of scaling up by the grid method.

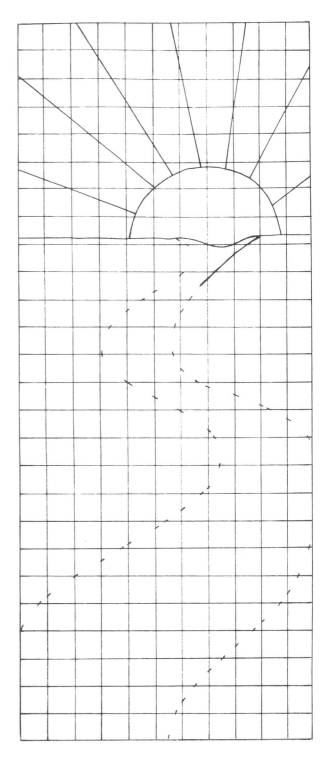

unfasten the corners carefully and put away the poster board for another use.

It helps to know what size squares are needed to bring the drawing up to the proper size, all the patterns in this book will note the size squares needed.

A more high-tech method is the pantograph. A pantograph is basically two pairs of sticks connected at the ends with a hinge and crossing each other to form a diamond shape. To change the scale, you change the crossing points. One end of the device is attached to the drawing table, the original drawing is placed under the hinged joint, and the paper for the enlargement is placed under a pencil at the other end of the stick. As you trace over the drawing at the bend a larger version comes out at the end. Don't ask me how.

The pantograph is not a very complicated device and with a little practice you can whip out a scaled-up drawing in short order. In the Appendix, you'll find plans for making your own pantograph. The only real critical part of the instrument is the scale. If you get it wrong, the tool will still be consistent, but results will be hard to predict at first.

Some copy machines are marvellous tools which can scale up or down at the push of a button, while relieving you of all that loose change in your pocket.

These machines enlarge by percentage, so if there is a grid on the drawing measure a square and calculate the percentage of increase needed. For example, if the squares on the drawing measure ¼ inch and you need ½-inch squares then the percentage of increase is 50 percent. They won't all be that easy, but knowing what part of the whole you need will get you close on the first try. The same works for any given dimension. If you know the overall length or width of the final object, then measure the length in the drawing. If it's only 25 percent of the length needed enlarge 75 percent. The rest of the dimensions will follow suit. If the machine will not enlarge enough in one go, make an enlargement of the copy.

Sometimes the machine will not use large enough paper to produce the whole drawing, so you might have to reposition the material in the copy machine to get a portion of the drawing you need. Then piece the copies together to make the complete drawing.

Double-Walled Vessels

The idea for double-walled vessels came from friends who were doing some very nice and elaborate double-walled pottery. All they did was roll out flat sheets of clay, turn them into cylinders of different diameters and fit one inside the other with a space between. They added a bottom and lid, cut designs into the outer wall, and had a very attractive pot. It was several years before I realized a similar principle could be translated into wood, and once I got started many variations began to present themselves. I put most of the ones that worked in this book.

Most wood containers either turned on a lathe, or formed into a box, such as a cabinet. A double-walled pot adds a third type, and frees you from both the spherical, single-walled shapes of a lathe and the angular box shapes of joinery. Double-walled vessels also let you use the band saw rather than the table saw or lathe.

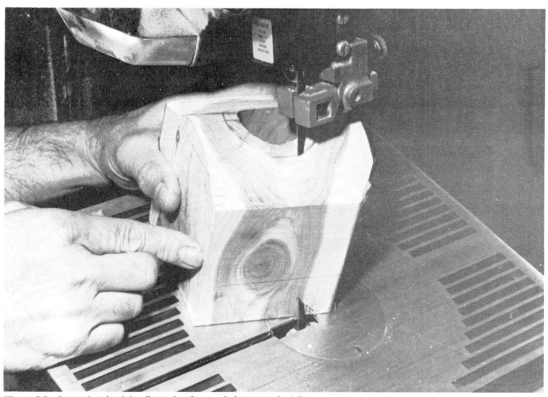

Illus. 30. Saw the inside first, before gluing or shaping.

Basically, you saw into a prepared chunk of wood (it could be anything from a laminated block to a raw log), and saw out the inside space to the desired shape (Illus. 30). Glue the entrance kerf shut; then shape the outer wall. This can be anything from a straight-sided cylinder to an asymmetrical cone to an angular shape with concave or convex sides (Illus. 31). You can also make any number of walls.

This is one of my favorite types of projects. You can make this from a limb trimmed off a tree, a block of laminated scrap, or even a piece of wood from your firewood pile. The point is not to be intimidated by expensive material so you won't be afraid to try something off the top of your head.

There are two aspects to woodworking: one is to follow technique and procedures to perfection; the other is to be adventurous and see what you can make work. I spend a lot of time doing the latter, though most of my good and consistent work comes from the former. But this is the type of project where both aspects of woodworking can come together. The technique is simple and, as you'll see, the variations endless.

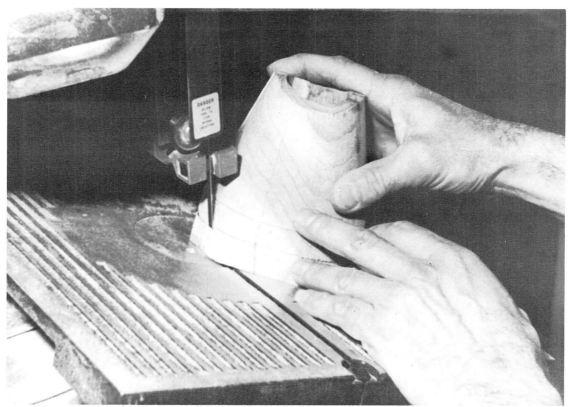

Illus. 31. If the top and bottom angles are the same, the piece can be sawn upside down, on the other side of the table.

Illus. 32. Use sawn off parts to saw a shape in the opposite direction.

Illus. 33. Sand the inside before fitting the bottom, as with this popcorn bowl.

Bamboo and Oval Flame Double-Walled Vessels

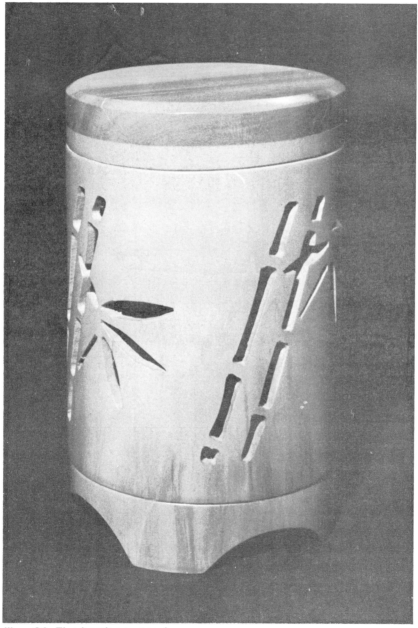

Illus. 34. The bamboo vessel.

The bamboo vessel starts with a 7½-inch-long piece of poplar log with the ends eyeballed square. Saw the log into a cylinder, at least 4¾ inches in diameter. With the sides parallel, stand the log on a flat table top and, with a framing square, square the sides with the table by putting small wedges under the log. Once squared, use a scriber (page 125) to draw a line around the bottom of the log, then saw along this line on the band saw. (If your eye is pretty good you should saw off just a sliver.)

Now, saw ½ inch off the top of the log (for the lid) and saw 1¼ inches off the bottom (for the base). If your band saw won't saw 7¼ inches deep, saw off the lid and base parts before sawing the log into a cylinder.

With a compass, draw a 4½-inch-diameter circle for the outer wall. Shorten the radius ¼ inch and draw the outside face of the middle cylinder. Shorten the compass another ¼ inch and draw the inner wall. Draw one more circle for the inside space, also with a ¼ inch less radius.

Saw out the outer wall first; then cut straight into the middle and saw out the inside space. To get the saw started into the circles straight, use a wedge to spring open the kerf just enough to get the saw blade to line up square (Illus. 36). The cut must be square in order to get good clamping

Illus. 35. The oval flame vessel.

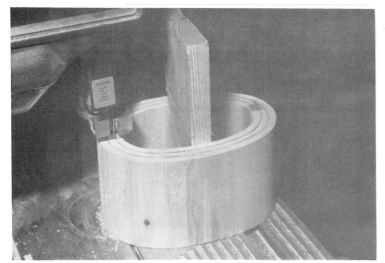

pressure and an almost invisible glue line.

Saw all three cylinders out, but only glue the entrance kerf of the inner wall. Two or three band clamps give the best results. Be sure to clean off excess glue from the inside before it dries, because it's hard to sand in there.

Saw three ¼-inch-wide rings off the middle cylinder, two for the top and one for the bottom spacers. Saw another ¼-inch ring off the top of the outside wall and keep it for the lid. To get the rings to fit snugly around the inner wall, lay them flat on the band saw table, holding the kerf closed, and pass the kerf through the saw (Illus. 37). This will shorten the ring and keep both surfaces parallel for a good glue job. After three or four passes you should have a good fit.

For the bamboo vessel we want a lid that'll fit down over the inner wall and be flush with the outside of the finished product. To make sure the spacer is even and ¼ inch all around, use the scriber to draw a line around

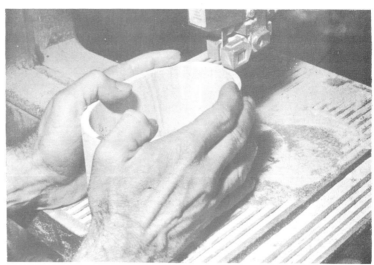

Illus. 37. To fit the outer wall, hold the kerf closed and pass it through the saw until it fits.

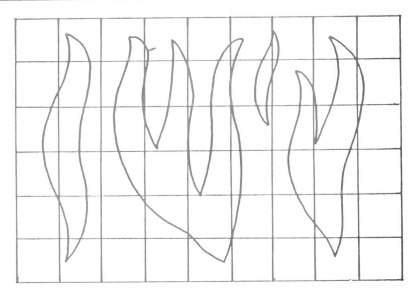

Illus. 38b. The oval flame takes four sections.

the cylinder as a guide for gluing. The bottom spacer, of course, goes on the bottom. With the rings in place you can paint or stain the inner wall for contrast.

Before you start cutting the bamboo design, remember curved sur-faces are very difficult to judge in distance. I always lay out a full-size pattern on paper (Illus. 38a–38b) and transfer it to the wood with carbon paper. Designs that run up and down the container are easy to deal with, but horizontal designs are much

Illus. 39. Drill holes in the design to allow a saw surface. Note the use of the bar clamp.

more difficult because the curve of the surface distorts their shape. A good way to check a horizontal design is to roll the pattern on a cylinder and view it as a curved surface to make sure it isn't too distorted.

The single most helpful tool in cutting the design is a bar clamp used as shown in Illus. 39. With the outer wall clamped firmly to the bench,

you can use drills, sabre saws, hacksaws, etc., to cut the pattern (Illus. 40). After the pattern is cut, fit the outer wall the same way as the rings.

Now, for the lid and the base. Fit the ¼-inch spacer around the protruding top ¼ inch of the inner wall (on top of the other spacer ring), glued only at the kerf. Use a piece of wax paper to separate the ring from

Illus. 40. Much of the design can be sawn with a jigsaw.

42

the wall. Now glue the ring from the outer wall to the spacer ring and glue the ½-inch top of the log to the top of the lid rings (Illus. 41). Done this way the lid can't help but fit quite nicely.

Glue the base to the walls, making sure to line up the grains. The base of the vessel has a cross cut (" + ") across the bottom to form the four legs (Illus. 34). This was done on the nose of the belt sander after the base was glued to the container. Round the edges between the lid and container and between the base and container lightly with sandpaper to accent the two lines. As with the entrance kerf, they can't be hidden, so make them an element of the design.

The oval flame vessel is even easier to make. Use the ovaler (page 123) to draw the shape, then cut the log to the outer shape and square it. Saw ⅜ inch off the top and the bottom. When the body of the container is glued together glue the bottom ⅜ inch of the log right to the bottom of the container, or cut it to fit inside.

This lid is to lay flat on top of the container, so glue the top ring flush with the top of the inner wall. Glue the top ⅜ inch to the ring. Cut a cleat in the shape of the opening and glue it to the inside surface so the lid will fit snugly and stay in place.

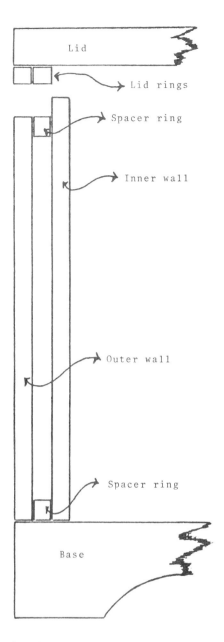

Illus. 41. The anatomy of a double-walled vessel.

Free-Form Vase

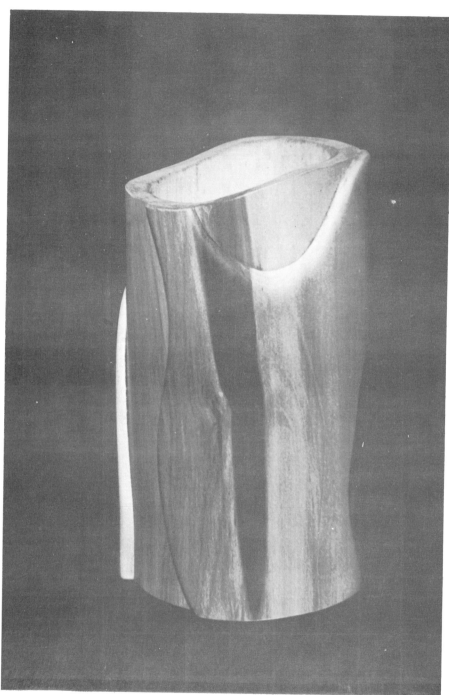

Illus. 42. The free-form vase. Saw the outer wall to any shape you like.

Another approach to double-walled construction is to leave out the space between the walls, giving you much greater freedom designing the outer wall. Freedom of design translates into free-form, which in turn translates into whatever you like. Free-form's big advantage is that nobody can ever say you're wrong.

A vase is a basic vessel. One of the problems with a vase, however, is that it must hold water. Wood of any kind does not like doing this, no matter what you seal it with, and the only real solution is to line the vase with glass. The best way to do this is to start with a water glass that is near the appropriate size and cut the inside space of the vessel to fit the glass. Cut the space so that the glass will slide in and out without any diffi-culty. Shape the rest of the vase around this. The vase in Illus. 42 was made of poplar. The outside diameter is 3½ inches, the height is 6¼ inches and the inside diameter is 2¾ inches.

Saw two cylinders; one, the inner wall (the actual vase), and the second for the outer wall. The outer wall should be ⅛-inch thick.

In this case the design is just free-form shapes sawn out, sanded and glued back onto the vase lining up the grains just as they were. You can use several individual pieces or one piece for the design. This particular design has two pieces.

Before you glue it all together, sand all the parts to the finished stage and remove any glue which squeezes out at the edges.

Hand Holding Cup

To carry the spaceless double wall further, perhaps beyond need, it can also be used to form a specific shape, in this case a hand holding a cup with the hand being the handle with which to hold the cup. The cup has no glass insert so its best use is to keep pencils and stuff from rolling around on your desk.

The cup is a straight-sided cylinder $2\frac{7}{8}$ inches in diameter and 4 inches high with a wall $\frac{3}{16}$ inch thick. The second wall is $\frac{1}{8}$ inch thick, and this is the handle ("hand") of the cup. This means that the log must be at least 6 inches in diameter.

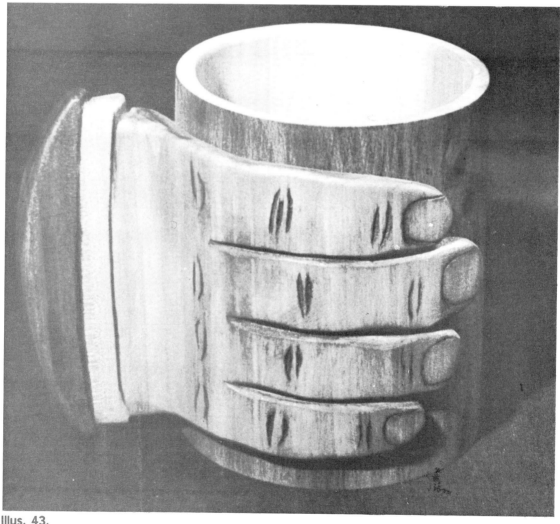

Illus. 43.

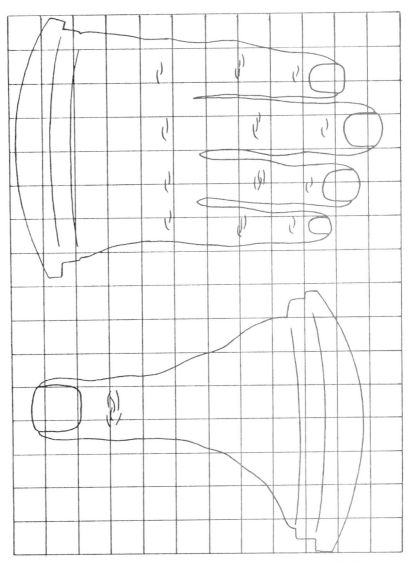

Illus. 44. The hand holding cup pattern may look out of proportion, but when rolled around a curved surface it comes out right. Enlarge to ½-inch squares.

One way to get the hand pattern is to tape a piece of paper around the wall of the cup and draw the outline of your fingers and thumb. The pattern can then be transferred to the wood. You can do most of this cutting on the band saw, but some will need to be done with a hacksaw or similar blade held in your hand.

With the shape sawn out you can add the fingernails and the knuckle wrinkles by making a light vertical incision along the line with a knife. Make a second cut with the knife at an angle about ¹⁄₁₆ inch from the first cut using enough pressure to reach the bottom of the first incision. This lifts a thin ribbon of wood, leaving a

Illus. 45. Apple wood cups were made to hold a glass insert for coffee or tea.

groove. Apply a dark stain and immediately wipe off. The groove will retain the stain and provide the contrast for the detail. A little sanding may be needed to clean up the edges before gluing the hand to the cup.

I have included a hand pattern (which should be enlarged to ½-inch squares) in case you'd rather use a pattern than your hand (Illus. 44).

This cup could be made to fit a glass liner and be used for your morning coffee (Illus. 45). I chose not to use it to drink from, figuring that would be too much of a hand-to-mouth situation.

Breadbasket

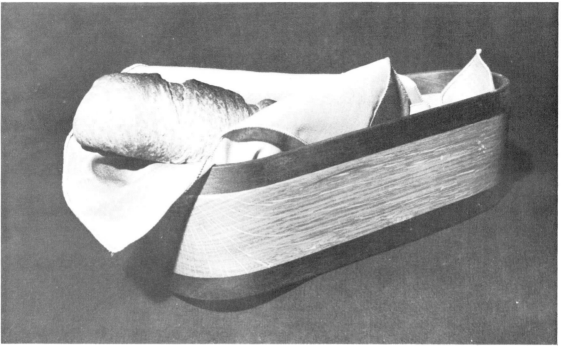

Illus. 46.

This is the most used basket at my house. It's also the simplest one to make. The breadbasket is made of mahogany and oak, but it will work just as well with other combinations of wood.

The basket requires two pieces of mahogany ($5\frac{1}{2} \times 14 \times 1$ inch) and one piece of oak ($5\frac{1}{2} \times 14 \times 2\frac{1}{4}$ inches). Glue one mahogany piece face to face on the oak for the top of the basket. Lay out the oval on the mahogany with a wall thickness of $\frac{1}{4}$ inch, and saw out the inside space first. The saw kerf should come in at the end grain and go perpendicularly through the basket wall, then curve over to the line marking the inner wall of the basket (Illus. 47a). This allows for a good flat gluing surface so the kerf becomes almost invisible when finished. Saw the inside and outside of the basket at a 6° vertical angle (page 25).

With the inside sawn out, glue the kerf and clamp it with as much pressure as you can muster, making sure the wood lines up exactly (Illus. 47b). When the glue dries, sand the inside of the basket to the finish stage. Now glue the second piece of mahogany onto the bottom of the oak, but be extremely careful to keep the glue away from the inside of the basket.

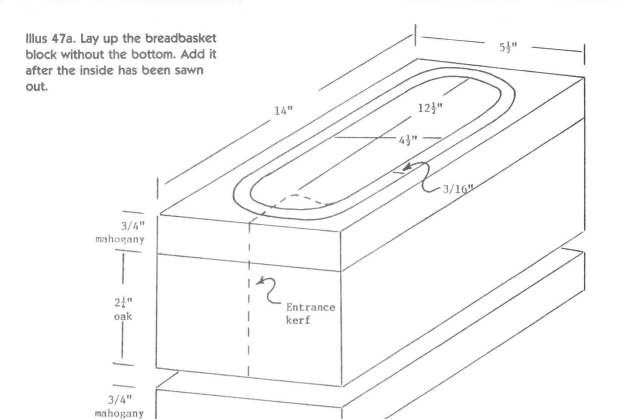

Illus 47a. Lay up the breadbasket block without the bottom. Add it after the inside has been sawn out.

5½"

14"

12½"

4½"

3/16"

3/4" mahogany

2¼" oak

Entrance kerf

3/4" mahogany

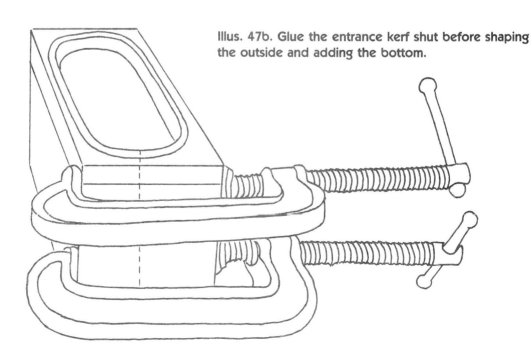

Illus. 47b. Glue the entrance kerf shut before shaping the outside and adding the bottom.

Finally, saw the outside shape of the basket, and sand the top piece of mahogany to vertical. This gives a top visual edge of about ⅛ to ³⁄₁₆ inch and a slight change in direction in the profile view, preventing the basket from appearing slab-sided.

A quick finish is salad bowl oil approved by the American Food and Drug Administration as a food additive. However, I don't much like the finish of salad bowl oil so I soaked mine in re-heated pre-boiled linseed oil. To do this, use a galvanized bucket half full of linseed oil and heat it on the kitchen stove until tiny bubbles begin to show. Soak half the basket at a time for about 15 minutes each. (Don't overheat the linseed oil.) The hot oil totally permeates the wood for a stabilizing and water-resistant finish. Wipe off the excess oil and give the basket several days to air out before use.

Muffin Basket

Illus. 48.

Variations on the breadbasket could go on ad infinitum. Here is one such possibility, the muffin basket. It uses the same material, but with one band of mahogany between two pieces of oak. With the added height the visual aspects change dramatically, but the technique remains the same.

Glue up the block in the same way as the breadbasket, then saw off the bottom (⅜ inch is the best width), cut out the inside oval and glue the kerf shut. Now glue the bottom ⅜ inch back just as it came off and shape the inside. The overall dimensions of the container are 4¾ × 8 × 5⅜ inches. Again, saw the inside and outside at a 6° angle (page 25).

It's called the muffin basket because it will hold a dozen muffins and the greater depth keeps the ones at the bottom warm until dinner time.

Illus. 49. Shaping the top of the muffin basket.

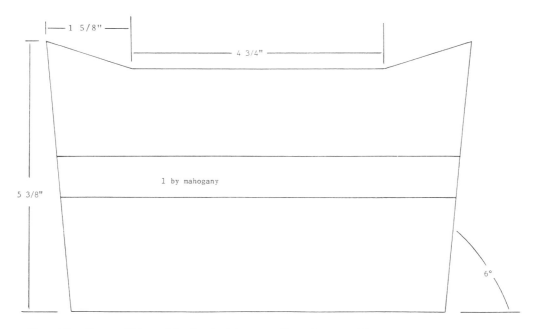

1 5/8"

4 3/4"

5 3/8"

1 by mahogany

6°

Illus. 50a. Use a 6° bevel in the inside as well as the outside.

Illus. 50b. Pattern for blocking out the muffin basket.

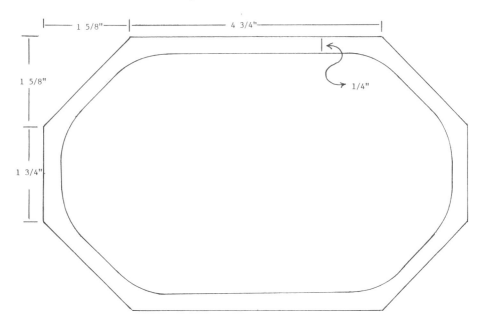

1 5/8"

4 3/4"

1 5/8"

1/4"

1 3/4"

Baskets with Handles

Illus. 51.

This basket is basically a horizontal arrangement. In its simplest form it's just an open-ended cylinder with one side shaped to form a handle (Illus. 52). For a more complicated basket you could saw out two cylinders and shape the smaller one for the basket and the larger one for the handle (Illus. 53).

Here's another possibility: saw out the outer cylinder and put it aside for the handle. Now saw off the ends of the inner cylinder, cut out the basket, and refit the ends. Finally, shape the handle and glue it in place.

Whatever you try, remember a basket must have a flat bottom, otherwise it'll roll over and play dead. So sawing a flat side for the bottom should be the first thing you do. After that you can fix the top and sides without any problems.

The basket and handle should be sanded to the finished stage before being glued together. They can also be stained separately before gluing. Overlap the handle at least one inch onto the basket for a good gluing surface.

The baskets can be as deep as your

Illus. 52. Saw the outside of the basket first.

Illus. 53. After the outside is shaped, saw out the inside, or bottom, of the basket; then the handle can be shaped.

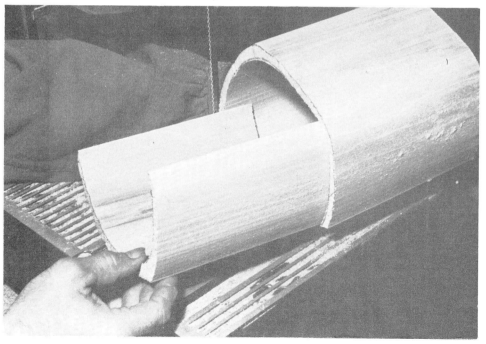

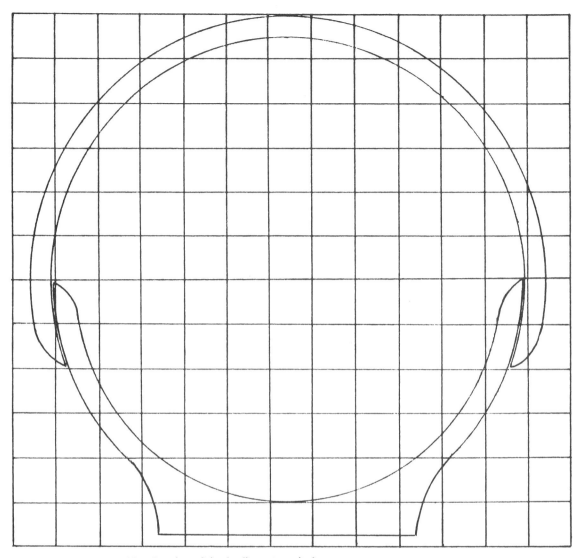

Illus. 54a. The round basket is a 6-inch diameter circle.

band saw will cut. You can extend the length if ends are used, since the ends are sawn off before the center of the basket is cut out. The wall thickness doesn't have to be more than ¼ inch, although you can vary the thicknesses of the baskets or handles, such as the "Not Quite Round" basket.

All the baskets shown here (Illus. 54) have the handles fitted onto the outside, but there's no reason you can't saw the handle from the inside of the basket. A basket with the handle fitted onto the inside rather than the outside? I'll leave the design possibilities to you.

56

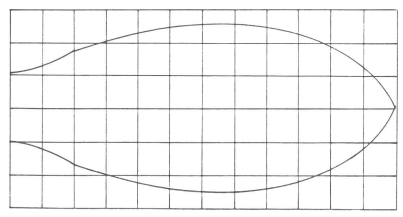

Illus. 54b (above). The handle pattern for the round basket is one-half the length. Enlarge to ½-inch squares and double the length to form both sides.

Illus. 54c (below). This basket is 6½-inches wide so a log of about 7 inches in diameter is needed. Enlarge to ½-inch squares.

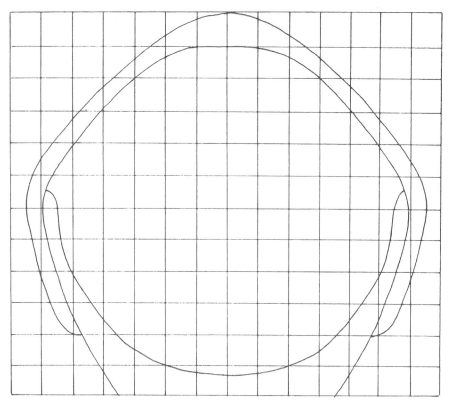

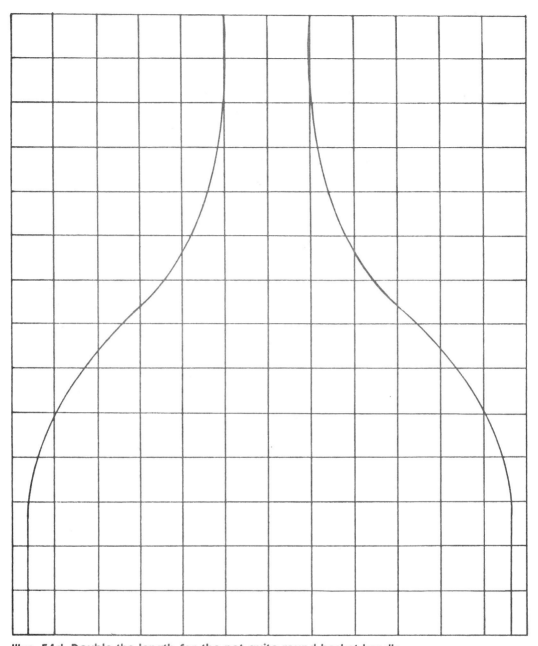

Illus. 54d. Double the length for the not-quite-round basket handle.

Folding Baskets

Illus. 55.

A folding basket is, in effect, a wooden spring using the natural flexibility of the wood in a way we don't normally think of. The results give a flat piece of wood a three-dimensional form.

The folding basket is an old idea I read about years ago in an English woodworking magazine. The idea is ingenuously simple. By sawing a continuous spiral in a flat piece of 1-inch-wide wood at a 4° to 6° angle (page 25) the edges of the saw cut can be sprung up, binding at about half the thickness of the board (Illus. 56).

All hardwoods I have used work well; even yellow pine works well but is fragile, especially where the handle meets the basket. The way around this, however, is to make the basket rungs ⅜ inch thick instead of the ¼ inch used with hardwoods. Whatever wood you are using *must* be free of knots. Knots will not spring.

Use a fine-toothed blade for this project. The idea is not to feel obligated to sand teeth marks from the basket rings, because it's just about impossible. Two things can help avoid sanding: have a lot of teeth on the saw

Illus. 56. Folding baskets made of pine, 6½-inches and 9½-inches in diameter.

blade; and resist the temptation to feed the saw too fast. It'll get a little boring sawing round and round, but it will soon be over, so don't rush.

The patterns are very hard to draw (Illus. 57). There are not grids on them because the best way, by far, to enlarge the patterns is the copy machine (pages 32–34). Transfer the pattern to the wood with carbon paper, being sure to include the handle pivot marks.

Cut the handle from the board first. The handle has two functions, one is as a handle and the other to hold the sides of the basket at their binding point. Saw the handle at 90°. It can be a different shape on the outside edge from the basket's shape (see the small round basket—Illus. 57a).

Illus. 57a. The round basket can be enlarged to any size of your liking, within reason.

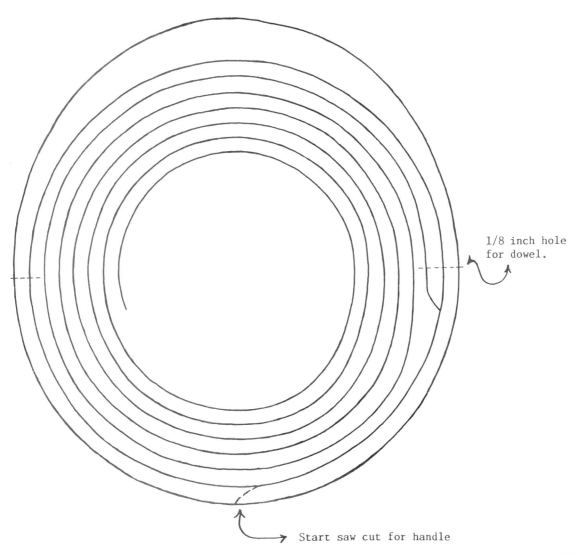

1/8 inch hole for dowel.

Start saw cut for handle

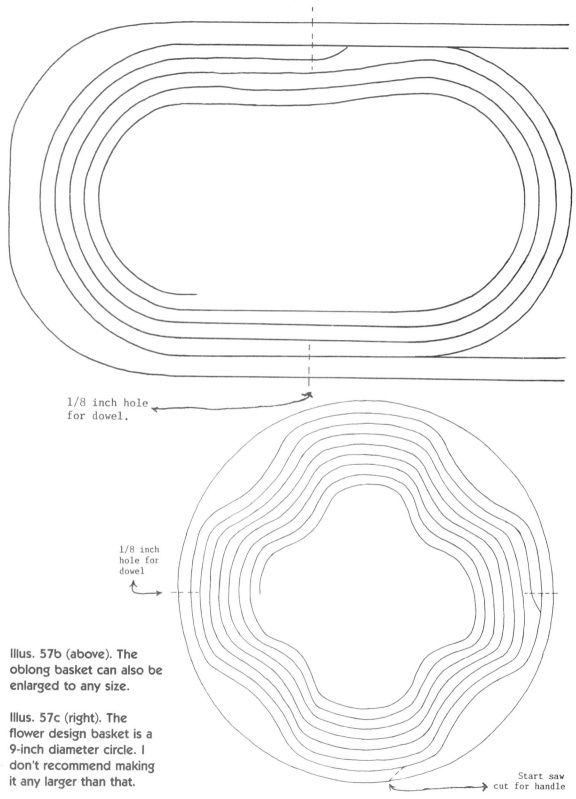

1/8 inch hole
for dowel.

1/8 inch
hole for
dowel

Illus. 57b (above). The
oblong basket can also be
enlarged to any size.

Illus. 57c (right). The
flower design basket is a
9-inch diameter circle. I
don't recommend making
it any larger than that.

Start saw
cut for handle

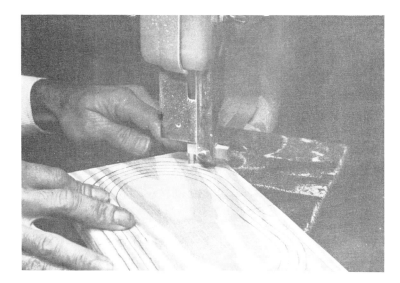

Illus. 58. Saw the handle at 90°, while the rest of the basket must be sawn at 4° to 6° from vertical.

After the handle is done, tilt the band saw table to either 4 or 6°. An angle of 4° will make a steeper-sided basket, while 6° will give a shallower one (Illus. 58). (Any angle over 6° will bind too soon and be flat, while an angle under 4° won't bind at all.)

Start the angle saw cut an inch below the point where the handle attaches. Saw continuously around to the end of the cut, then turn the saw off and slowly back the wood out.

Lay the handle flat against the basket, and pin it with ⅛-inch dowel. With the handle in position on the basket, line up the marks and drill a ⅛-inch hole through the handle, the first (outermost) rung, but not quite through the second (Illus. 59). Now slip the dowel into the hole. Do the same on the other side, but drill through the handle and only part way through the first rung and insert the dowel.

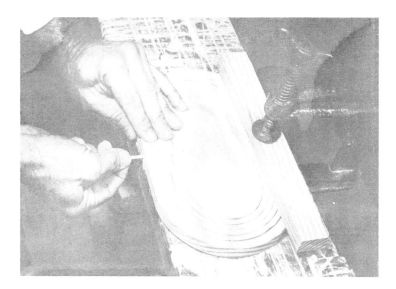

Illus. 59. Fitting the ⅛-inch dowel through the handle and into the basket.

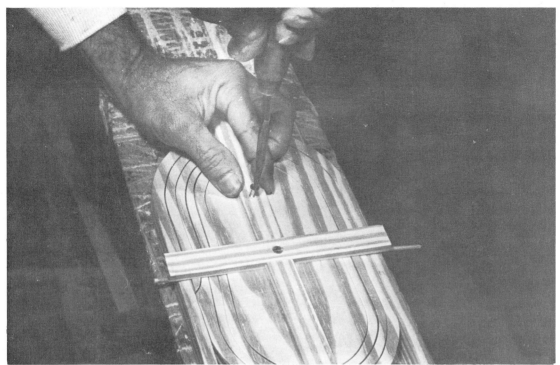

Illus. 60. Screw ¼-inch-thick strips onto the bottom for the handle to push against when opened.

Illus. 61. Mark the length to cut the handle.

With the basket and handle temporarily pinned together turn the basket upside down and screw on strips of wood (¼ × ¾ inch), long enough to cross the length and width of the basket (Illus. 60). The strip which will support the ends of the handle should cross the basket uninterrupted, while the other strip should be in two pieces. Together, they form a brace that holds the basket flat when closed and supports the handle to hold the basket open. Use ¾ inch #6 wood screws to secure the strips to the bottom of the basket.

Open the basket fully and mark the length of the handle. Cut the handle a little long (to allow for sanding) and make sure the basket will be extended fully when the handle is in the upright position (Illus. 61).

Remove the dowels and sand the basket and handle. Assemble the basket for the last time, putting a small amount of glue in the dowel holes that do not go all the way through the rung. This keeps the dowel in position as the basket is opened and closed.

Oils and waxes make the best finishes. Varnish or shellac is too thick and tends to gum up the works. I recommend filling a tray or baking pan with boiled linseed oil and soaking the entire basket for a few minutes, or even a few days. The pan can also be placed on the kitchen stove on a low flame and cooked for 10 minutes or longer, but keep an eye on it. This gives the oil deep penetration and results in a fine low-luster finish. The basket should then be left to dry for a couple of days. Oil-base stains can also be used with good results prior to the oiling.

Tankard

Illus. 62.

When someone I know is deserving of a gift I usually make a tankard. Maybe it's because the tankard is a bit of antiquity, not to mention nice looking. Or maybe it's because it's easy to make and will hold a twelve-ounce can of your favorite beverage. I always go for the utilitarian approach.

The tankard is made of poplar and mahogany (Illus. 63a). Saw a 4½-inch-high poplar log to a 4-inch di-ameter; then cut ½ inch off the top and ¾ inch off the bottom.

Take a 3½-inch piece of 1-inch-wide mahogany and glue it between the top ½ inch and the remaining 3¼ inches of poplar. Saw out an inside diameter of 2⅝ inches square with the top. Now glue another piece of mahogany and the remaining ¾ inch of poplar to the bottom and saw the outside shape to a 4-inch-diameter at the bottom with a 6° bevel (page 25). It is easiest to do this with the tankard upside down on the saw table, using the bottom as the line to saw to.

With the tankard shaped and sanded, make the handle from 1-inch-wide mahogany (Illus. 63b). You can add a little chip carving for decoration if you wish and glue it to the tankard with epoxy (Illus. 64). Either varnish or oil will give a nice finish.

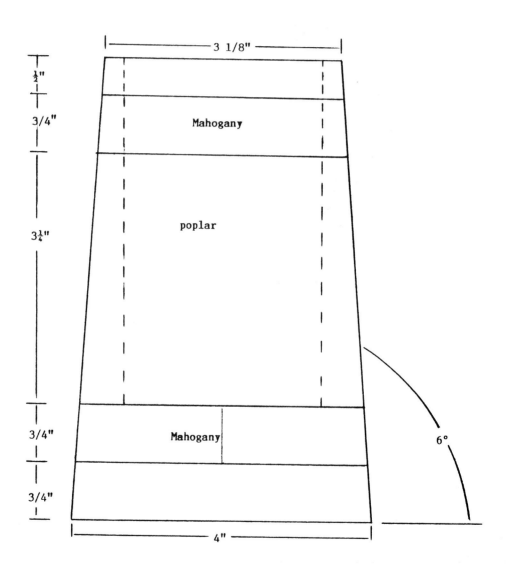

Illus. 63a. The tankard is 6 inches in overall height and will hold a 12-ounce can, so you can drink without getting your fingers cold or anyone knowing what you're drinking.

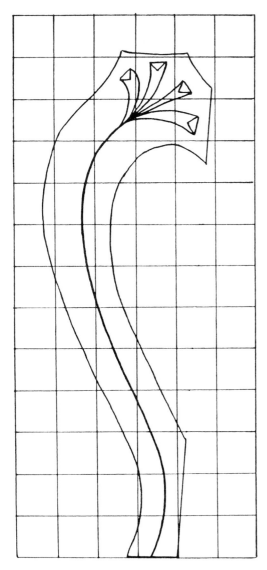

Illus. 63b. The handle pattern.

Illus. 64. A web clamp is the best way to glue the handle onto the tankard.

Hardwood/Plywood Vase

Illus. 65.

This vase uses a technique which you can use in your own designs. As you can see in Illus. 65, part of the vase below the plywood bevels out and part bevels in. This could occur several times in one design, giving the vase a wave effect. The bevels could be the same or they can increase and decrease as the shape rises. It's a fun idea to play with.

For this vase you'll need a 5-inch length of log at least 4½ inches in diameter (Illus. 66). Square the ends and saw 1 inch off the top. Then saw the center out of this piece at a 40° bevel (page 25). Glue the kerf shut and saw the outside to the same bevel. Now take the lower part of the log and saw out its center at an 8° bevel with a 3⅞-inch diameter at the top. Saw the outside using the same bevel, to a 4½-inch diameter.

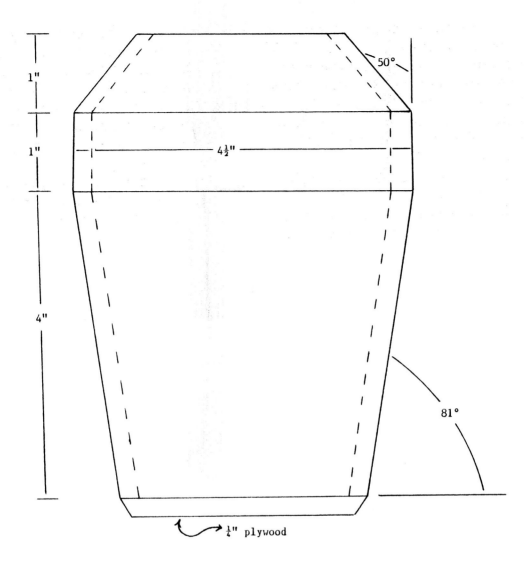

Illus. 66. The basic vase shape can be changed to fit any glass insert for holding flowers.

Cut a 1-inch-thick piece of plywood, or other contrasting wood, at 90° with an inner diameter of 4 inches and an outer diameter of 4½ inches. Sandwich this ring between the top and bottom portions. Use a ½- or ¼-inch piece of plywood for the bottom of the vase as well.

Line up all four pieces with all the entrance kerfs, glued together, on one side. The vase can be sanded and finished now with oil or varnish.

In Illus. 65, the top opening of the vase is shown as 2¾ inches. This is the diameter of the glass I used for the insert so the vase could be used for flowers. If you are going to use a glass insert, measure its greatest diameter and make the opening of the vase accordingly.

This combination technique has many possibilities and I sincerely hope you investigate them all.

Ring Stacking Projects

Illus. 67. The little brown jug, sawn from 2 by yellow pine.

Illus. 68. A stacked bowl of yellow pine.

Illus. 69. The ring stacking sphere.

Illus. 70. Compound curves and shapes
are possible with ring stacking. This is a
13-inch fir vase.

This stacking of rings is a good method for getting a shape that curves in both directions: up and down as well as around. The different shapes and sizes you can create are wide-ranging, but sawing out all those rings at different angles can seem a never-ending task. Once you have all the rings glued together, however, it's over quickly. Stacking rings is not a new idea, but it's fun and your band saw will do it very well.

Draw a line profile using a vertical center line and horizontal lines indicating the thickness of wood you intend to use (¾-inch, 1½-inch, etc.) (Illus. 71a). From the horizontal lines you can pick up the bevel of each ring with a bevel gauge and take it directly to the band saw. The vertical center line gives you the radius of each ring, both inside and out, at any point along its depth.

Saw the inside of the rings at the same bevel (page 25) as the outside or square them off, as in the Jug design (Illus. 71b). The inside shape depends on what you want it for. A lamp base only needs a wiring hole through it, while a vase or cookie jar would need the inside shape about the same as the outside. (In the case of the cookie jar, sand out the inside before gluing on the bottom.)

It's a good idea to number each ring. This helps a great deal when gluing time comes. Also, sometimes you can saw smaller rings from the inside of larger ones. Keep this in mind when laying out, it can save you some wood.

Gluing up large works can be hazardous to your mental health. Keeping the rings all in line while dealing with bar clamps and clamping pads is a little like chasing baby pigs. To avoid this, glue the object up in sections of three or four rings first; then glue the sections together.

The finished product will have a lot of end grain, which is good and bad. You can arrange the grains into patterns, such as all annual rings going up, or down. The trouble with end grain is that it's hard to sand. The belt sander makes things easier but in the end it's just rub-a-dub-dub.

Illus. 71a. Draw the shapes at half-width and take the bevels from the drawing to the band saw.

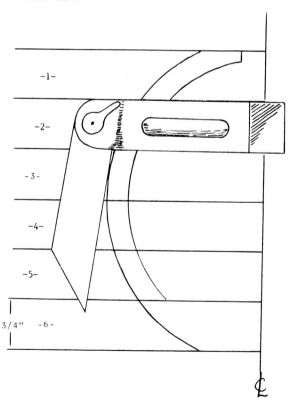

-1-

-2-

-3-

-4-

-5-

3/4"   -6-

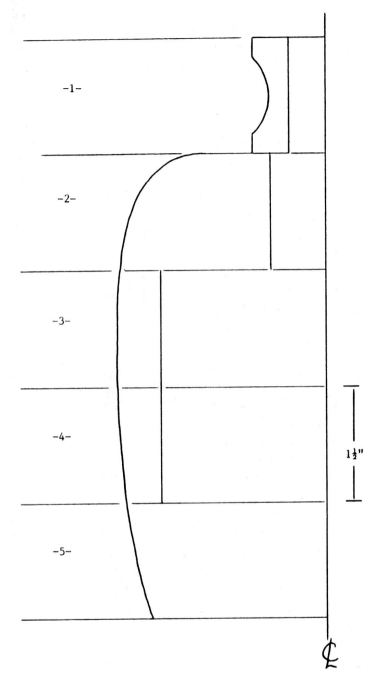

Illus. 71b. Ring stacking can produce shapes from spherical to compound curves. Make the jug from five layers of 2 by yellow pine; the insides of which have been sawn out square. Remember not to saw out the center of layer 5.

−1−

−2−

−3−

−4−

−5−

$1\frac{1}{2}"$

℄

Loon Chest

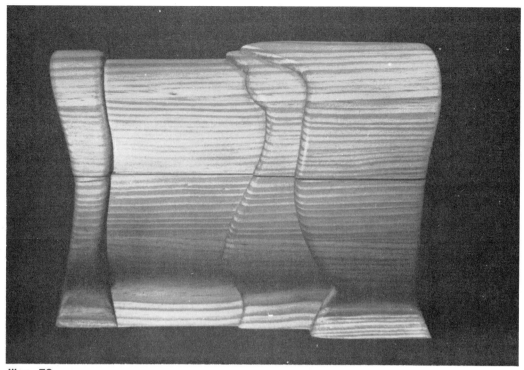

Illus. 72.

Chests are similar in technique to containers, except they're horizontal. Square a log, cut off both ends and put them aside. Saw out the inside space, with the entrance kerf on the bottom of the chest. Glue back the ends where they came from and saw the outside shape of the chest. The chest can then be stood on its end or held firmly on its side and sawn open. Hold the lid and chest together, shape the ends, and add the hinges and you're done.

In the case of the loon chest saw the shape from five layers of 2×8 yellow pine 10 inches long. Saw 1¼ inches off each end and cut out the inside shape, gluing the kerf shut afterward. Saw two ¼-inch outside layers off also and use them for the loon pattern. These layers are only the length of the chest without the ends, but that's all that's needed.

Now, hold the ends in position on the chest and use the scriber (page 125) to draw the shape. Saw them to shape and glue in place.

Sand the chest to the finished stage and saw the loon pattern from the outside layers and glue in place. The loon pattern runs all the way around the chest; that is, the loon in front is the same as the loon in back (Illus. 73). The two breaks meet at the top of the chest. However, saw the two separate patterns (Illus. 75) out in one piece so there is no glue line and nothing to fit. You can even out any excess or shortage at the bottom. Part of the function of the pattern is to cover the glue seams on the ends.

At this point what you have is a kind of hollow log with a loon on it, and this would be a good time to varnish or oil it. Now all you have to do is lay the chest on its side, saw it open, and add the hinges. The cut should be about 4¼ inches from the bottom of the chest. This line can be drawn down the side using the scriber.

The tray is held up by ¼ × ¼-inch cleats cut to the width of the chest and glued inside the ends (Illus. 74). You can make the tray itself from the piece sawn from the inside of the chest. Stand this piece on end and saw it in half. Then saw ¼ inch off each end, and saw out the middle in a "U" shape. Sand it down and glue the ends in place.

Illus. 73. The back of the loon chest looks the same as the front, except for the hinges. Note the pillow blocks added to the right hinge so the two hinges will be in line.

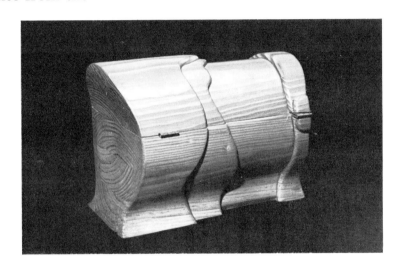

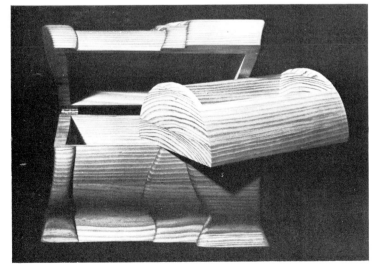

Illus. 74. Make the tray from the inside space of the chest.

Illus. 75a (below). The loon's back is cut on the outer wall, and the front from the middle wall. Enlarge the pattern to ½-inch squares.

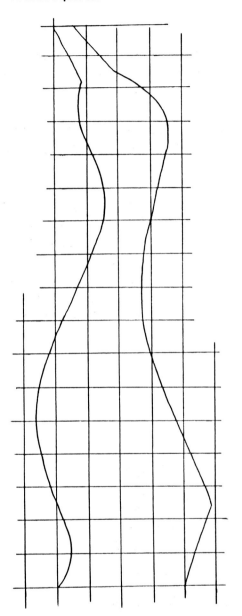

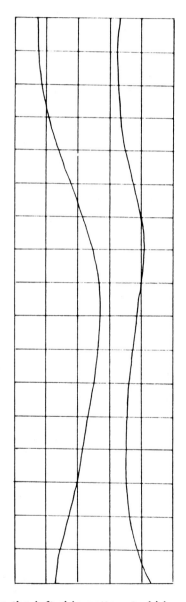

Illus. 75b (above). Use the left side pattern to hide the glue line where the end is glued into place. Enlarge to ½-inch squares.

Poplar Chest

The poplar chest seems to smile as it sits on my wife's dresser. User friendly, you might say.

Make the chest from a 6-inch-diameter log, 7½-inches long. Saw ¾ inch squarely off each end of the log and keep it for the ends of the chest. This makes the overall length 6 inches, an easy thickness of poplar to saw on my band saw.

Take the remaining log and saw 4½-inch-diameter circle out of the middle and glue the entrance kerf shut (Illus. 77). Saw the outside shape and fit the ends by holding them in place on the chest and tracing the chest's shape. Saw the ends to that shape and glue them in place. After the glue is dry, sand the chest fairing the ends into the chest.

Now, stand the chest on its end and saw the lid off. Hold the lid and chest together and bevel the ends at 6° (page 25), then add the hinges.

Make the tray from the piece sawn from the inside of the chest (Illus. 78). Stand it on end and saw it in half; then saw ¼ inch off each end. Saw out the middle in a "U" shape and glue the ends in place. The tray sits on two ¼-inch-square cleats glued to each end of the chest.

Illus. 76.

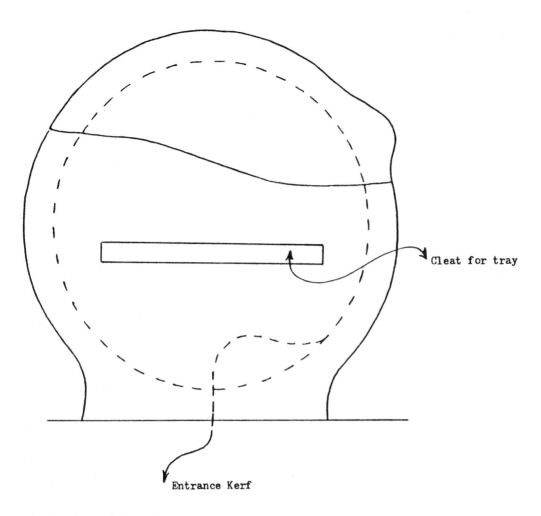

Cleat for tray

Entrance Kerf

Illus. 77 (above). Saw the poplar chest from a 6-inch-diameter log.

Illus. 78 (right). Make the tray from the inside of the chest.

Nut Bowl

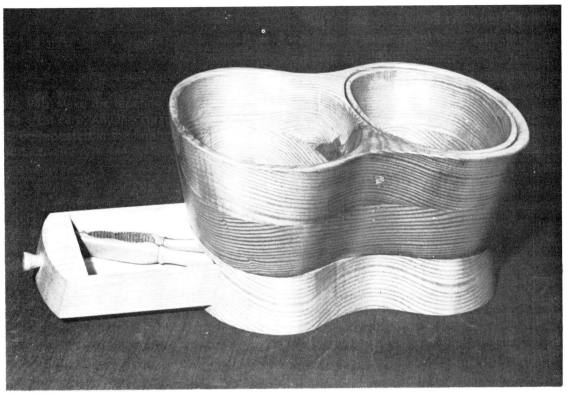

Illus. 79.

If I could give the same Christmas presents to the same people year after year, I think the nut bowl would be it. It's fun to make, has few parts that move, people examine it in hopes of finding secrets, and it's practical. What more could one ask?

Basically, the bowl is three 9-inch lengths of 2×8 yellow pine. The two upper pieces form two oval-shaped bowls, with one bowl having an insert, or "nested bowl." The nuts go in the single bowl and the shells are dis-

posed of in the nested bowl, which can be lifted out and emptied. The lower piece has a drawer that holds the nutcracker.

Make the bowls first. Use the ovaler (page 123) to draw the shape and glue two pieces of the pine together (Illus. 80a). Saw out the inside of both ovals and an entrance kerf at each end. Glue the kerfs shut. The outside of the nut bowl is then shaped and both the inside and the outside are sanded to the finished stage.

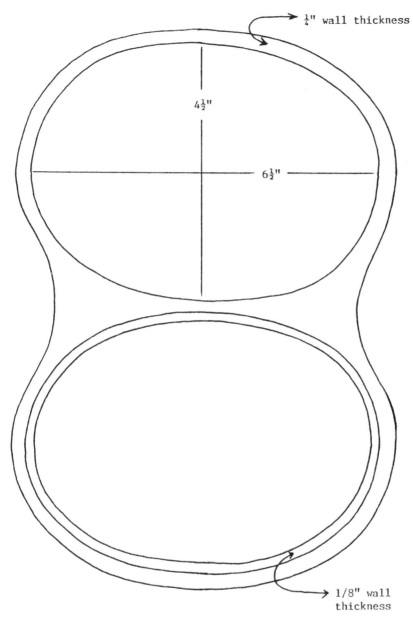

1/4" wall thickness

4½"

6½"

Illus. 80a. The nut bowl is two 6½-by-4½-inch ovals laid side by side. Make a separate entrance kerf for each oval.

1/8" wall thickness

The nested bowl is made from one of the blocks sawn from the inside of the nut bowl. Saw ¼ inch off the bottom and cut out the inside of the bowl to about ³⁄₁₆-inch-wall thickness. Sand the inside; glue the bottom in place and sand the outside. The bowls can then be set on the third piece of 2 × 8 and the outside shape (Illus. 80b) drawn, sawn out, and sanded to fit the bowls and form the base (as well as the bottom of the bowls).

Make the drawer by sawing off the

82

sides of the bottom, leaving ¼ inch at the narrowest part of the shape (Illus. 80c). Lay the center block on its edge and saw the drawer block out. Put the drawer block aside and glue the base back together; then glue the bowls down to the base. To make the drawer, saw ³⁄₁₆ inch off both sides, then cut out the drawer space and glue back the sides. A wooden golf tee glued into a ³⁄₁₆-inch diameter hole makes a great drawer pull.

The finished product can be oiled or varnished.

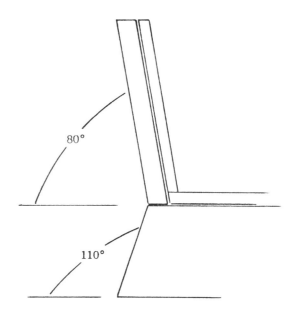

Illus. 80b. Saw the inside and outside of the nut bowl at the same angle.

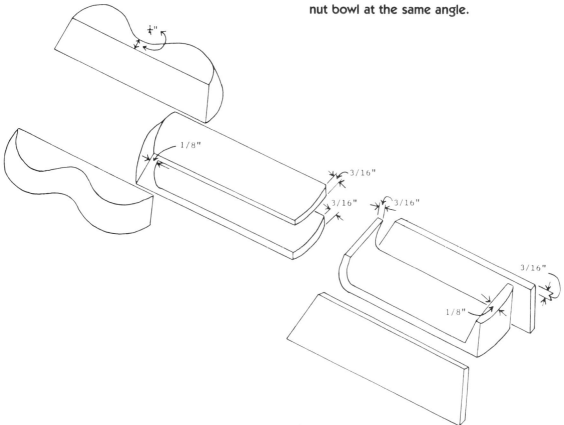

Illus. 80c. Shape and sand the nut bowl before sawing out the drawer.

Lap Desk

The lap desk is an old colonial favorite which still has a great deal of usefulness today. Except for the ¼-inch plywood bottom its construction is of 1 by clear yellow pine. The pine is stained a dark walnut and to keep from using any metal, it uses a simple and effective knuckle hinge, keeping its colonial functionalism (Illus. 82). You'll need 50 inches of 1 × 6 clear yellow pine, an 8-inch length of ¼-dowel and a 10¼ × 13 × ¼-inch piece of plywood.

First, saw two 14-inch lengths of pine and edge join them. Next, saw a 12¼-inch length of 1 by 6 and rip off a 3-inch width for the back. Use the remainder to make the front piece, at a bevel of 10° (page 25).

Make the two sides from the remaining pine. Lay them out at a 10° bevel as well, the 3-inch-high portion at opposite ends. Head to toe, as it were. Saw the sides to shape; then rabbet each end to receive the front and back. Glue the two sides, the front and back together, clamp them (check for squareness); then set it aside.

Now, sand down the top and lay out the pencil groove and knuckle hinge. A ⅛-inch band saw blade will saw a ¼-inch radius—in theory. In practice, however, you'll find a 5/16-inch radius much closer to reality. Another case of lowered expectations. Be that as it may, the easiest way to lay out the radius for the hinge curve is the end of a 5/16-inch dowel. This will give you a perfect radius in just the right place. Before you cut out the hinge, drill the dowel pin position ⅜ inch behind the hinge and centered in the edge (Illus. 83). I started this hole with a ¼-inch brad-point bit and drilled to its maximum depth; then changed to a 6-inch-long twist bit to complete the 4-inch hole depth. Use a router for the pencil groove, and then saw the knuckle hinge using a ⅛-inch 15-tooth blade on the band saw.

With the desk top in two pieces, sand the knuckle hinge to round the edges. This will allow the lid to raise and lower without binding. Drill the dowel pin holes on the lift-up part of the lid a 64th over so the ¼-inch dowel will fit tightly into the fixed

Illus. 83. Use a dowelling jig to drill the holes for the dowel pins, which will hinge the lid.

part of the top and loosely in the movable part.

Check the smoothness of the hinge movement by slipping the 4-inch lengths of dowel pin partway in place and lifting the lid. If there is some binding you will be able to see where it is and take appropriate action with the sandpaper.

Now, sand the base of the lap desk; then fit and glue the ¼-inch plywood bottom place. Once the glue is dry sand the plywood flush with the sides of the base. Round the edges slightly to tuck it under the desk. Round the corners slightly, as well as the corners of the desk top.

Finally, fit the top and the base together. The top should lie flush on the desk with the same amount of overhang on both sides. Screw the fixed part of the lid to the desk. (Use 1-inch #8 wood screws.) Counterbore and plug the screws. The movable part of the lid can now be removed from the desk and the two parts stained. After the staining, drive in the dowel pins flush with the edge of the top and touch up with a little stain.

The finish may be varnish, lacquer, or wax. Na-Nor Bowling Alley Wax or Johnson's Paste Wax results in a very hard finish that will get shinier with each coat. It is also very hard to buff by hand, so cut a piece of wool to fit your vibrator sander and you'll finish in no time at all.

Illus. 84. Exploded view of the lap desk.

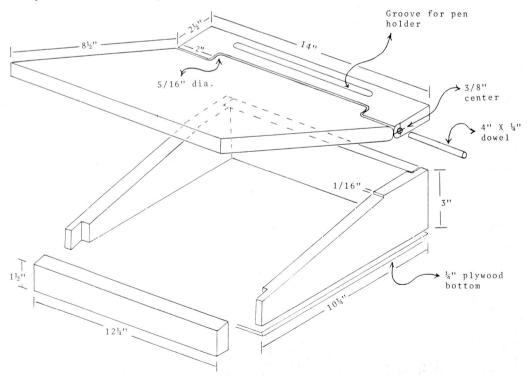

Vertical Stacked Planter

Vertical stacking opens up a whole variety of possibilities. For the planter, what you want to do is make a box the right height and width, but without a top or bottom. From this box you'll saw the inside and outside shape of the planter.

Make the box from mahogany and yellow pine laid out as shown in Illus. 87a. Use 1 by on the inner and outer layer, alternating the two species of wood.

Make each of the four walls of the box first. Glue the inner layer to the outer layer, making sure the tops and bottoms line up and the inner piece is in the dead center of the outer one. Leave ¾ inch on each side, and make sure you clean off any glue that

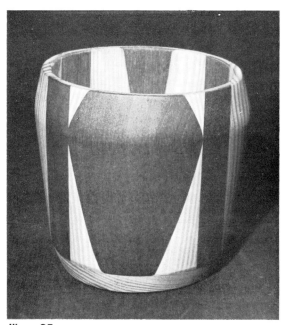

Illus. 85.

squeezes out into this space. When you've done this for all four walls, you can glue the box together. This'll form the blank from which you'll saw the planter.

Saw it out with a 5° bevel (page 25) on the bottom and a reversed 5° bevel at the top (Illus. 87b) and you'll find mahogany diamonds on two sides and pine diamonds on the other with each diamond flanked by the opposite wood. Fit a bottom and you're done.

You can vary the kinds of wood used, the outside shape, the blank,

Illus. 86. A yellow pine box was used for this planter, with interesting results.

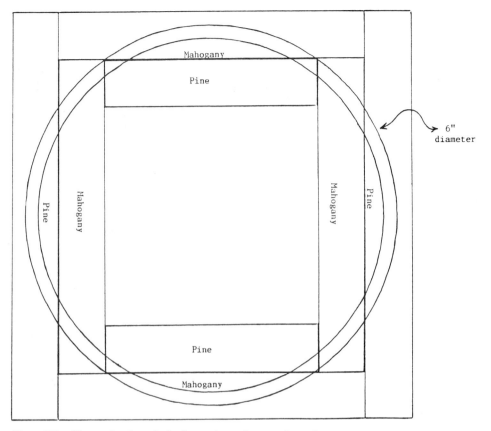

Illus. 87a. Since the box is hollow, there is no place for a compass point. Use this template (enlarged to a 6-inch diameter) to lay out the shape.

the thickness of the wood, or the way the corners of the box are joined. Any of these will affect the outside pattern of the planter (Illus. 87b). The main reason I'm glad I came up with this idea is that the pattern only reveals itself with the last saw cut. This is unlike most woodworking projects where the end results are known from the very beginning and the results hold no surprise when the job is finished. Here the results can be unpredictable, but never disappointing.

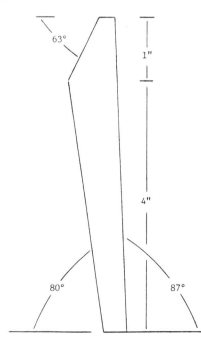

Illus. 87b. Any variation in angles or heights will produce alterations in the pattern.

Chicken Box

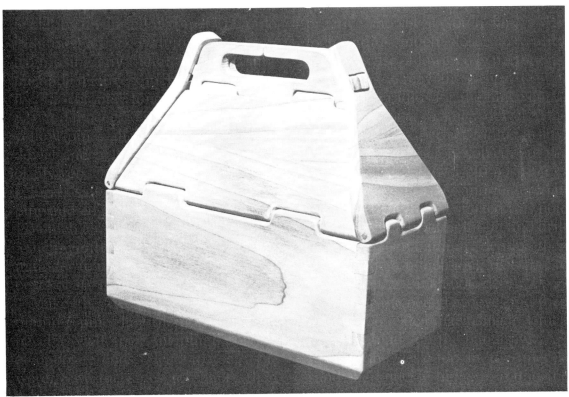

Illus. 88.

This box doesn't look like a chicken, sound like a chicken, or walk like a chicken. It's called a chicken box because my wife brought home some barbecued chicken one evening in a paper box that folded in this fashion. The chicken was good but the box was fascinating so I ate the chicken and kept the box with the idea of translating it into wood.

It is an interesting project that uses the box, or finger joint (page 24). It also takes the knuckle hinge to an extreme never before considered. The result is a lunch box, tool box, or even a purse, which'll attract attention.

The basic dimensions of the box are 12 × 5½ × 10-inches high, and it's made of ½-inch poplar.

Edge join the poplar to a width of 11¼ inches and a length of 36 inches. Lay out all four sides completely, including the finger joints (page 89a), the knuckle hinges, and the handle. When cutting the pieces above the hinge, cut out the tenons but not the mortise until after the box is assembled. This will ensure that the mortises are in the right place.

Now saw apart the four sides and drill ³⁄₁₆-inch holes (with a doweling jig) for the dowel pins. Next saw the

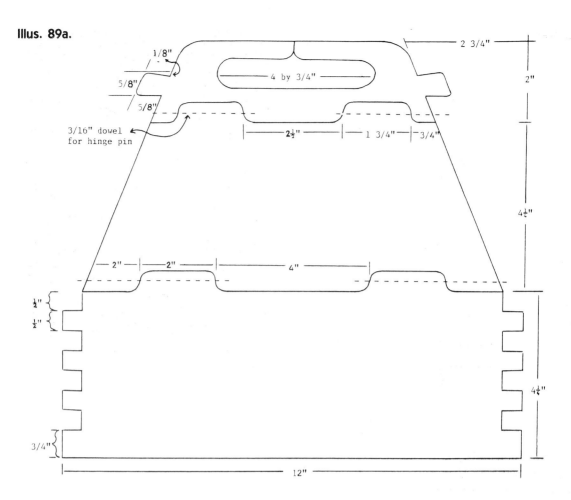

knuckle hinges and the finger joints (Illus. 90). Round all the edges of the knuckle hinge so that it will work easily. The hinges don't have to swing 180°, but just enough for them to open and close.

Assemble the box part of the project and fit the bottom. Glue the bottom to the box and saw it to a 30° bevel (page 25), using the glue line to saw to. You can also fit the bottom to the inside of the box or even rabbet it if you prefer. I just like it on the bottom with the bevel.

With the box assembled, fit the top part of the ends. With the ends pinned in place, swing them up so they lean against the tabs of the handle and mark their location and shape. Since the mortise is small, $1 \times 5/8$ inch, I recommend cutting it the old-fashioned way—without electricity; that is, with a knife and chisel. You'll need a small bevel on top of the mortise to allow it to slip over the tabs. This is so small a bevel that it is best to cut a little and look.

Once the ends swing up against the sides and slip over the tabs, you can take a pencil and mark the shape of the ends, leaving at least 3/16 inch alongside the mortise.

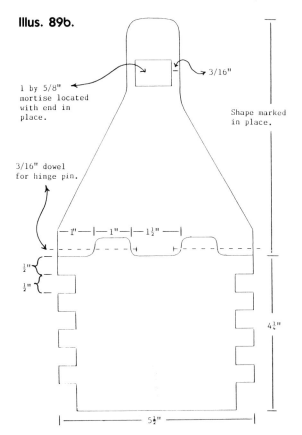

Illus. 89b.

1 by 5/8"
mortise located
with end in
place.

3/16"

Shape marked
in place.

3/16" dowel
for hinge pin.

1"—|—1"—|—1½"

½"

½"

4¼"

5½"

Illus. 89. Lay out the sides (Illus 89a) and ends (Illus 89b) on 36-inch by 11¼-inch by ½-inch stock. After sawing apart, drill the ³⁄₁₆-inch holes for the hinge pins.

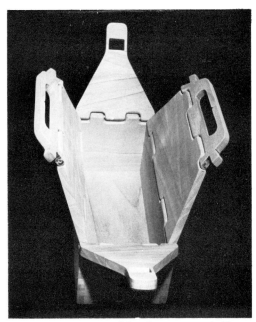

Illus. 91. The box with wings spread. The knuckle hinge allows the box to open and close.

Illus. 90. Cutting the finger joint on the band saw. First cut down the sides of the fingers; then saw out the excess.

Horned Sake Cask

Illus. 92.

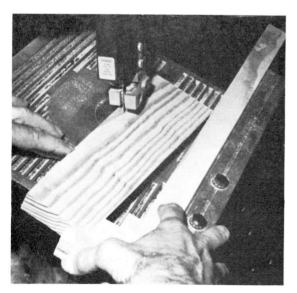

The horned sake cask has an elegant simplicity designed into a practical object and I couldn't resist making it. More important, though, the project illustrates how to use the band saw to cut bevelled tapers, which will fit together quite nicely without sanding or planing. You can use this technique not only to make the sake cask, but also lamp bases, drawer fronts, cabinet doors, bedposts, planters, chests, and even a hot tub or your very own Conga drum. Take out the taper and you can make cylindrical or oval shapes.

The sake cask is 22½ inches at the horns and 5¾ inches across the bottom. The six short pieces of the cask's body are cut from 12-inch-long 1 by 4 yellow pine. The two horns are cut from 22½-inch-long 1 by 6 yellow pine (Illus. 94a). Cutting the longer pieces on the same tapering jig as the shorter ones will give wider dimension at the bottom of the horns. This, in turn, gives the cask its oval shape and saves you from having to make another jig. Whoever made the first sake cask might very well have had this in mind.

Make the tapering jig first. The jig (Illus. 94b) is two pieces of ½-inch

Illus. 93. The tapering jig cuts the taper while the band saw table takes care of the bevel. Turn the jig and the stock around to cut the second taper (see Illus. 95).

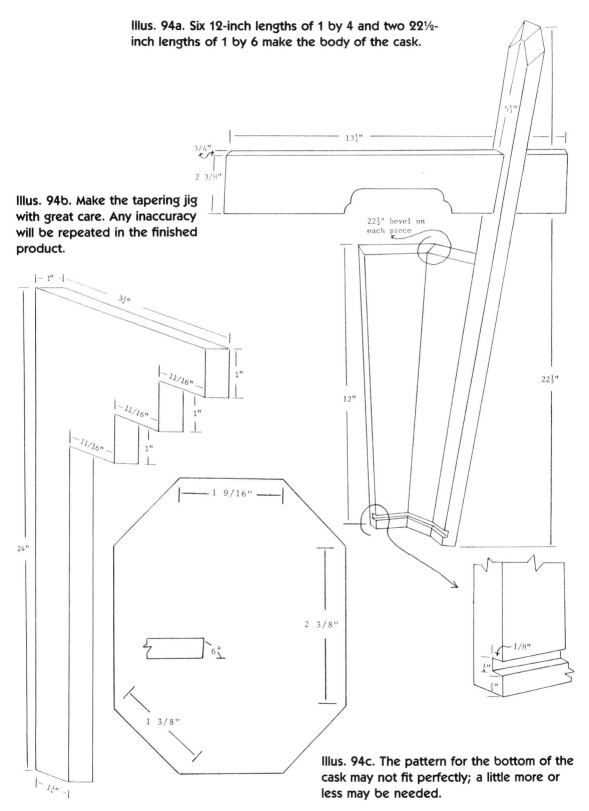

Illus. 94a. Six 12-inch lengths of 1 by 4 and two 22½-inch lengths of 1 by 6 make the body of the cask.

Illus. 94b. Make the tapering jig with great care. Any inaccuracy will be repeated in the finished product.

Illus. 94c. The pattern for the bottom of the cask may not fit perfectly; a little more or less may be needed.

plywood. This will give a 1-inch thickness, good for working the ¾-inch stock needed for the cask. Lay out the jig so the first step-in is the distance you want taken off each side. Then make the second step-in exactly the same (Illus. 94b). The stock you use will all have to be the same length and width if you want it to have the same taper, and will have to sit on the long end of the jig, or the taper won't be what you had in mind. So make

this part of the jig long enough for what you need. It should also be thicker than what you're cutting, especially when you're cutting a bevel, so the wood won't ride over the jig.

Use ¼-inch plywood for the bottom of the cask, with a ⅛-inch rabbet, ½ inch from the bottom edge of the sides. Cut the rabbets in the walls, before the taper, using a stop clamped to the cross-cut fence and another stop clamped to the saw table. The

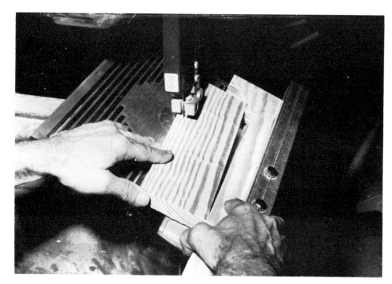

Illus. 95. The taper jig sawing a taper, with the head facing away.

Illus. 96. It's best to glue up the cask in two pieces. A little jig such as this will insure good clamping pressure.

bottom of the cask is a hard piece to fit, so I have included a pattern (Illus. 94c) which, if it doesn't fit exactly, will be close enough for corrections to be made.

With the jig made and the stock cut to the needed dimensions, it's time to saw. Let the jig hold the taper while the band saw table holds the bevel (page 25). Set the bevel at 22½° (as in Illus. 94a), and use the second step on the jig. Cut all the taper/bevels on one side of the stock first, and saw the first taper with the head of the saw away from you (Illus. 95). When all the first sides are cut, then flip-flop the jig and stock for the second taper and bevel (Illus. 93).

With all the pieces cut, they can be

Illus. 97. Finish gluing with a web clamp.

glued together. Don't try to glue them all together at once, it's too maddening. Two at a time in the gluing jig is the best way (Illus. 96). It may seem a little slow but it's a small price to pay for your mental health.

While the glue is drying on the short pieces, you can cut the mortise on the horns and make the handle from a piece of 1 by 4 yellow pine, following the dimensions in Illus. 94a.

The lid is the last thing to make. Before breaking into the pine it's best to make a template from plywood or even cardboard. Cut the material to lie snugly between the horns and on top of the sides. Draw a center line from horn to horn and cut the material along this line, cutting the template in half. Lay half the material back in position and reach inside the cask with a pencil to trace the shape of the cask onto the template material. Then cut out the shape and do the same on the other side of the cask. Butt the template together at the center line and draw the shape on the yellow pine lid material. Reduce the size by ⅛ inch on all sides so the lid will sit inside the cask about ½ to ¾ inch below the top, and saw it at a 6° bevel. The handle for the lid is a 2¼-inch length of ¾-inch dowel glued to the lid with a ¼-inch dowel connecting the two.

The sake cask on which this one was based was, as is most Japanese woodwork, black lacquered, but I liked the cask so well without any finish I almost left it as it was. As always, the choice is yours.

Band Saw Art

SAWING IT OUT

As woodworking projects go, band saw art is pretty simple. And, as with most things that are simple, it's open to your imagination, and a lot of fun. You can use these projects for cabinet doors, table tops (under glass) or wall decorations. The basic technique is to transfer a simple line drawing to a board, saw out the pieces of the drawing like a puzzle, assemble the puzzle, (using different woods or wood stains to create contrast) and glue the pieces back together on a piece of plywood. Complications to follow.

You'll get a striking result by using two layers of 1 by with the grain of one layer at 90° to the other, or two layers of different kinds of wood, a dark variety (walnut or mahogany) and a light variety (oak or poplar or yellow pine). Hold the two layers of wood together with a water-soluble glue (Elmer's school glue) with a piece of poster board glued between two layers of wood. After sawing out the pattern split the two pieces apart, clean off the paper and glue, and assemble all the pieces. This two-layered procedure yields two complete pictures, both of which can be finished with excellent results.

A three-layer block can also be used to increase the variety of interchangeable pieces, but this should be used only for very special pieces because usually the results don't outweigh the waste of good wood and the extra hassle in gluing up the block. It might be better to select the pieces which you would like to be a third variety of wood and pattern them off.

In some of the designs you'll need a shutter, or filler, piece. When too many saw kerfs go in too many directions you may have a gap somewhere. The remedy is to pick the most convenient piece and, out of scrap if possible, make a new piece large enough to take up the space. Most of the designs here don't require a shutter.

In looking at some of the designs it's hard to tell where to make the first saw cut, so I've put little arrows along the line to saw first. Sometimes, though, you'll have to back the wood out and start the same line again from the other side. There are many possibilities for sawing out the patterns, so if you see a better one than the one I indicated, use it.

The first step is to glue up the two layers of wood to form the desired-size block with the poster board in between. If you are gluing up crossing grain as shown in Illus. 98, cover the horizontal grain with a thin coat of water-soluble glue and lay the poster board on; then cover the poster board with water-soluble glue so it's ready for the two pieces of wood which make up the vertical grain layer. Give these two pieces together with a permanent glue, such as Titebond, on the edges.

Lay one piece of vertical grain onto the poster board and clamp it to the horizontal piece.

Lay the second vertical-grain piece on the glued cover paper and clamp it lightly to the horizontal piece. Now you can clamp the two vertical-grained edges tightly together for the permanent glue. You can also tighten the clamps holding the vertical and horizontal pieces together. Allow the glue to dry.

Use carbon paper to transfer the scaled-up pattern to the wood. You can now saw the design on the band saw, carefully following the lines of the pattern.

When the pattern is completely sawn assemble the pieces so that you can keep track of what goes where; otherwise it can, in fact, become a puzzle. When assembled, take a knife and separate the two layers of wood at the paper (Illus. 99). As each piece is separated, reassemble the pieces, keeping the vertical and horizontal pieces separate and face up. Remove the paper from the pieces by either washing with warm water or by sanding. I usually hold them to the belt sander. With all the noise and paper flying, it seems faster.

With the pieces cleaned and assembled, lay them side by side and interchange the pieces: vertical grain with horizontal grain, or light and dark wood (Illus. 100). Any number of pieces can be changed. It is simply a matter of switching them around to find the best advantage the wood has to offer.

Once you've decided on the pieces,

Illus. 98. This is the layout of vertical and horizontal grains.

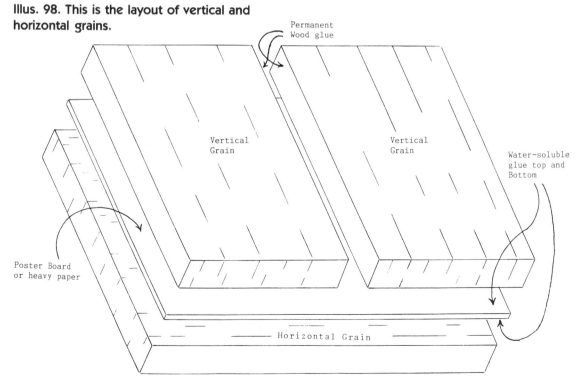

Permanent Wood glue

Vertical Grain

Vertical Grain

Water-soluble glue top and Bottom

Poster Board or heavy paper

Horizontal Grain

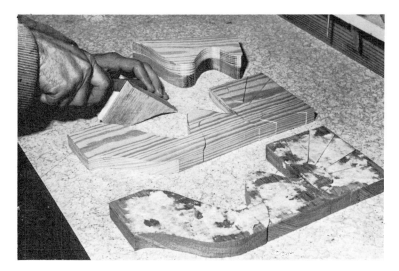

Illus. 99. Splitting the pattern pieces apart.

the next step is to shape the edges by sanding. You can do most of this shaping on the nose of the belt sander clamped to the workbench. This will open the lines of the surface of the work and give the work definition, as well as a soft, padded look. This is a freehand operation and the best approach is the "cut-and-look" method. Some pieces will want long, sloping curves, others will want only short, slightly rounded edges, and many pieces will want a changing shape on the edges. One suggestion that may help on your first piece of band saw art is to cut, using the sander, a ¼-inch bevel on the top edge of all the pieces first. This will let you see how the surface lines open up and help you see what edges to slope further.

Once the edges have the shape and look you want, sand all the pieces by hand to remove all the sanding marks and smooth all surface edges. (It is also a good idea to dampen all the pieces with warm water, let them dry, and sand again with 220 grit sandpaper.)

Illus. 100. Rearranging the horizontal and vertical grains to get the best advantage of the wood.

If you want to stain anything, do it before gluing. It is best to stain the individual pieces, surfaces and edges, and allow them to dry (Illus. 101). This way, you can use different stains without running the risk of getting unwanted stain on another piece. After the stain is dry, sand the pieces lightly, with a fine sandpaper, to enhance the figure and to lighten the high spots (giving a shading effect).

To get away from the restrictions of wood tones, use some colored stains, as in the sailboat piece. Minwax makes a red, blue, green, and white stain which works very well. These stains are not always easy to find, so a good alternative is artist's acrylic paints. These paints are pastes that come in tubes and are thinned with water to the desired consistency. Squeeze out a small dab onto a piece of scrap wood, load your brush with water, and mix. The more water you add, the thinner the paint and the more the wood figure will show through. The thicker the paint, the darker the tone and the less figure. Mixing on a piece of wood will give you a good idea of what it will look like when applied to the work. Remember the color will tone down when varnished over. When the acrylic dries, sand it to smooth out any brush strokes or to lighten the color.

Another technique for changing the character of yellow pine is to burn the surface of the wood with a propane torch, then vigorously wire brush it to remove the char. This can be a little messy, though. Burning darkens the early wood, while leaving the late wood mostly unaffected. This will enhance yellow pine, leaving an overall dark appearance and bringing out the texture and contrast of the smoothly sanded wood. But if you haven't tried this burning business before, you might want to practise on a piece of scrap first. The longer you burn, the darker and deeper the relief—to a point.

When the staining and coloring is

Illus. 101. The edges of each piece should be stained, as well as the surface. All staining should be done before the pieces are glued to the ¼-inch plywood back.

complete, the work is ready to be glued to the ¼-inch plywood backing. Give the back of each piece a coating of permanent wood glue and assemble the pieces on the plywood. Make sure they all fit together snugly and lie squarely. Clamping the individual pieces together is not necessary, but some down pressure to hold the pieces to the plywood is helpful. To do this best, lay another piece of plywood on top and weigh it down with a brick or something. Squeeze out any excess glue between the

Illus. 102. The frame is 1¼-inch thick strips of I by mitred and glued directly to the edges of the picture.

pieces and carefully remove it before the glue dries.

After the work is glued and thoroughly dried, sand the edges to remove any excess glue and to square the edges before framing. I usually use 1¼-inch strips of yellow pine with mitred corners for the frame. Fit the strips and glue them directly to the edges of the picture, clamping them until the glue dries (Illus. 102). Sand and stain the frame before gluing.

The final step is to oil or varnish the finished work. Tung oil is a good finish which is easy to apply and which imparts a soft luster to the work. Apply it with a cloth, and use two coats. Let the first coat dry 24 hours before doing the second coat.

The uneven surface of the work does not lend itself to applying varnish or shellac with a brush. However, polyurethane varnish is available in spray cans and works very well. Several thin coats sprayed on the work will give a high-gloss finish, and the spray is forced deep into the cracks giving a good even finish. The high gloss can be reduced by rubbing with fine steel wool after it's dry.

A good source of designs for band saw art are stained-glass design books. The patterns usually require the addition of some lines and the alterations of others to allow them to be sawn on the band saw, but you'll get the idea. Children's coloring books can also be a source of inspiration. The two main things to remember in drawing your own designs are: 1) you must be able to saw it out on a band saw, and 2) the fewer lines the better.

ART PROJECTS

THE SUN AND RIVER (OR ROAD)

This is a simple one to make. It works well with either a single or double layer of wood. It's a good one to start with because it's not too big and has all the difficulties you are likely to face on the more complicated ones. You'll need a shutter piece (see page 96) for the sun's rays. The sun can be cut from a third piece of wood, such as end grain. If enlarged to ½-inch squares, the overall size should be 5½ × 13 inches.

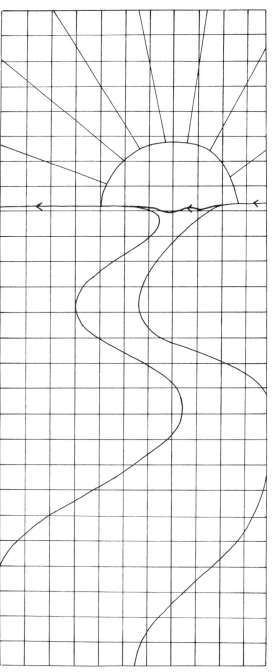

Illus. 104. The Sun and River.

Illus. 103.

THE LYNX

The Lynx rates high in my book. The pattern is visually straightforward, simple, with nothing there that doesn't need to be. It's not the easiest to make, however. The little pieces that make up the eye are difficult to shape and fit back together, but at least you won't need any shutters. The best color scheme is to use a dark and a light wood, with the dark as the background. I used two layers of yellow pine for the background, with the grain vertical, burned, and wire brushed. The Lynx should be enlarged to ½-inch squares. This will yield a 11 × 14-inch Lynx.

THE OWL

I must have made a dozen of these things. It seems as though everybody who does not collect owls knows someone who does. I usually use two layers of yellow pine and alternate grain direction. I also alternate light and dark stain, starting with light at the forehead with dark eyebrows, light eyes, and so on. Starting with a

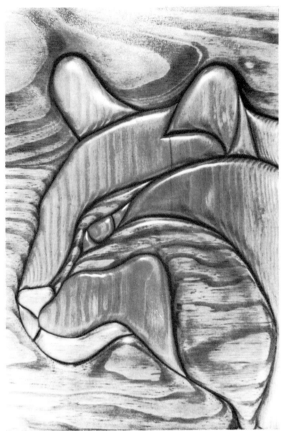

Illus. 105.

dark stain on the forehead also works well. The owl will be 10¼ inches × 7 inches if enlarged to ½-inch squares.

Illus. 106.

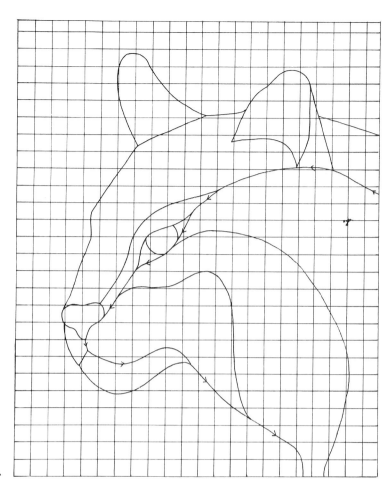

Illus. 107. The Lynx.

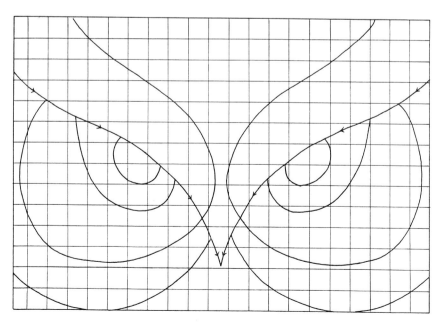

Illus. 108. The Owl.

THE SAIL

This is a striking piece with the sails colored and the background left natural. It is fairly easy to do until you get to the people sailing the boat. I used the man at the mast as a shutter piece to help take up slack which occurs between the boat and the sails.

Saw out the water first, then saw up the bow of the boat and on up the line dividing the two sails. Once the picture is in two pieces, the rest is easy. If enlarged to ½-inch squares the overall size will be 9¾ × 13¼ inches.

Illus. 109.

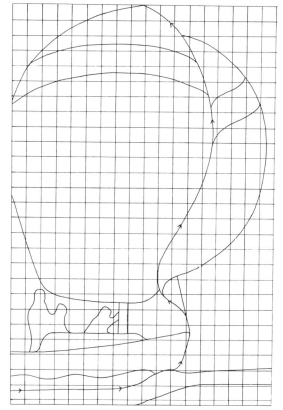

Illus. 110. The Sail.

CATTAILS

This is a fairly simple two-tone piece which works best with a light and a dark variety of wood (such as mahogany and oak). If the darker wood is the background you have the effect of receding distance; if the lighter wood is the background, you get a silhouette effect. Either way the results are quite handsome. The proportions can be changed by drawing two patterns side by side and using all or part of the second pattern. The design should be laid out on ½-inch squares which will give an overall size of 7⅛ × 13 inches.

Illus. 111. Cattails.

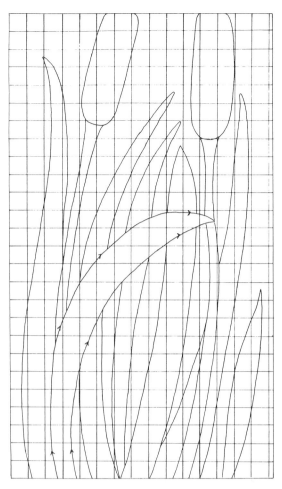

Illus. 112. The Moorish Idol.

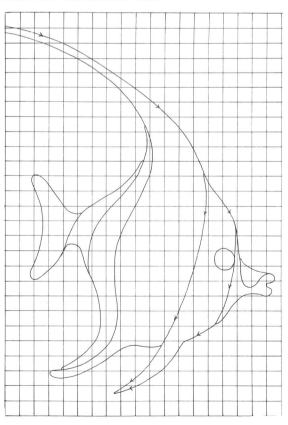

THE MOORISH IDOL

The wavy figure in yellow pine would make a good underwater background and could be left natural or burned and wire brushed to gain texture. The fish should be stained with color. (The Moorish idol is a colorful fish.) The segment of the fish just in front of the tail may need to be a shutter piece. If enlarged to ½-inch squares the overall size will be 11 × 14 inches.

THE STILL LIFE

This is supposed to be a little abstract. The vertical strip background is a little hard to see on the grid, so I have marked them with little ticks. The design should be enlarged to ½-inch squares which results in a picture of 7 × 14 inches.

The best color scheme is to leave the background in natural yellow pine with the bottle and glass a medium tone. The part where the bottle and glass overlap and the table should be a darker tone.

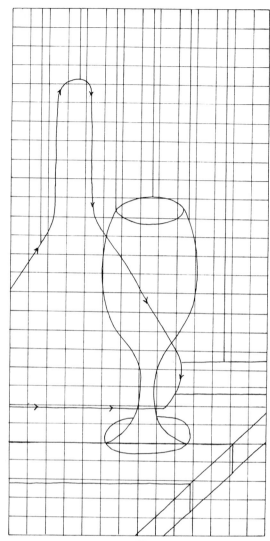

Illus. 113. The Still Life.

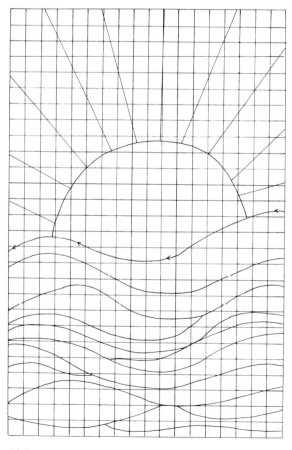

THE SUN AND OCEAN

Flowing water always works well in band saw art. Colored or wood-tone stains could be used on this piece, with natural and medium tones for the sun and rays and natural, medium and dark tones in the water. If the design is scaled up to ½-inch squares it will be 9 × 13½ inches.

Illus. 114. The Sun and Ocean.

THE TOUCAN

Enlarge the pattern to ½-inch squares, which will yield a 7 × 13-inch Toucan. It looks more birdlike if the body parts and head are stained with color and the background is left a natural wood tone.

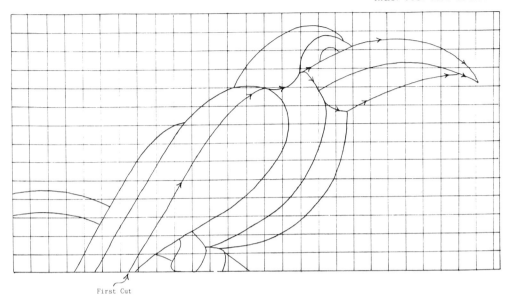

First Cut

THE CAT

This is one of my favorites. It's easy to make and very striking. Little coloring is needed, but the background is best stained dark with the cat's face light to medium and the eyes natural. The overall size will be 7 × 14 inches if enlarged to ½-inch squares.

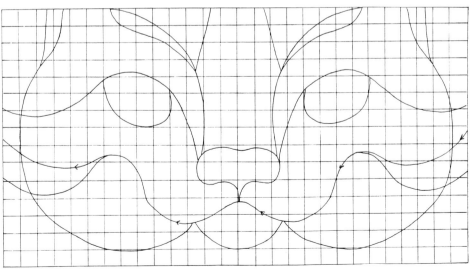

Spice Cabinet

Illus. 117.

Illus. 118.

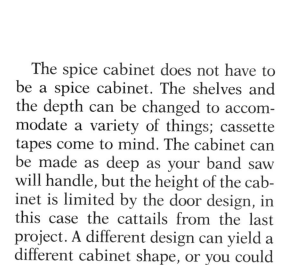

The spice cabinet does not have to be a spice cabinet. The shelves and the depth can be changed to accommodate a variety of things; cassette tapes come to mind. The cabinet can be made as deep as your band saw will handle, but the height of the cabinet is limited by the door design, in this case the cattails from the last project. A different design can yield a different cabinet shape, or you could use the negative (Illus. 118).

THE CATTAIL DOORS

This design is two of the cattail patterns put together. One pattern has been turned over so that they face each other. You can turn the pattern over by laying it on a piece of carbon paper with the carbon side up. Draw

108

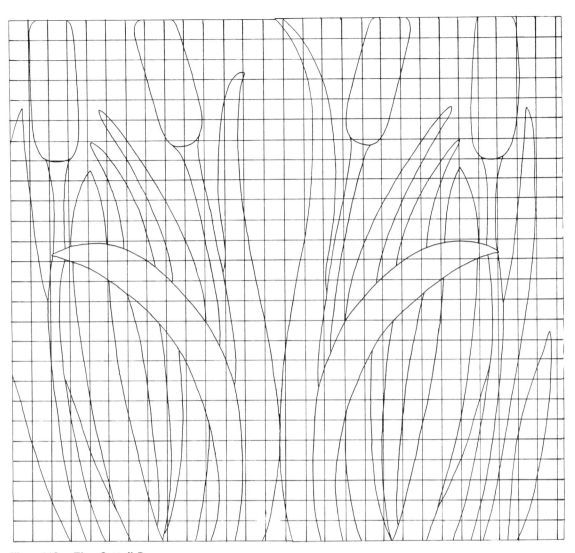

Illus. 119a. The Cattail Doors.

over the pattern, then look on the back side of the paper and there's the image, visible and turned over.

I altered the design slightly, from the previous chapter; the tall leaf in the middle goes all the way from top to bottom to provide a place for the doors to open. I made my doors sepa-rately, but the design could be laid up as one piece.

The cornice at the top of the cabinet is a simple wave design which is glued up without the plywood backing. The double cattails will be $14 \times 12\frac{3}{4}$ inches when enlarged to $\frac{1}{2}$-inch squares.

The first thing to do is build the doors (Illus. 119a). They are the primary feature of the cabinet and will also determine the final dimensions (in other words, you're building the cabinet to fit the doors). The doors are completely framed, including the top piece which is not attached to the doors but to the cabinet. The bottom of the doors should extend below the cabinet to act as door pulls. This eliminates the need for a distracting handle in the design.

When the doors are done, measure them and set the dimensions for the cabinet. Use 1 inch thick clear yellow pine for the cabinet frame. Rabbet the corner joints and shelf slots. (This should all be done on the band saw.) Use ¼-inch plywood for the back of the cabinet and glue it to the back of the frame. The shelves are also ¼-inch plywood and they simply slide into the slots without glue, unless they fit too loosely, in which case a little glue may be appropriate. Sand the plywood back flush with the sides of the cabinet and then round it off so it folds behind the cabinet.

Hinge the doors to the cabinet next, making sure the top outside corners of the doors land at the top outside corners of the cabinet. With the doors hung and swinging nicely start fitting the top piece of trim. It's a good idea to remove the doors to glue the top trim piece in place.

The cornice is the last piece. Saw it from two horizontal layers of yellow pine and mahogany (Illus. 119b). After the pieces are sawn, shaped and sanded, lay them flat on a plywood backing, glue and clamp them as if you were edge joining two pieces of wood. Then glue the entire assembly to the top trim piece on the cabinet.

Illus. 119b. This is only half of the design for the cornice. It should be flipped over at the center line to lay out the second half. Enlarge to ½-inch squares.

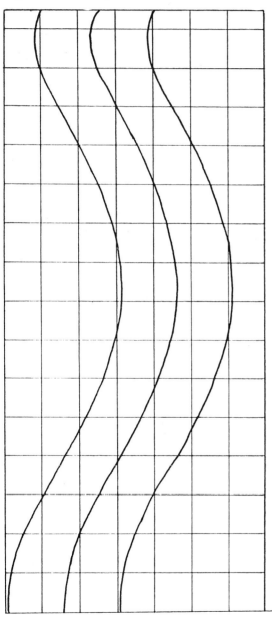

Put the doors back in place and make any little adjustments before you apply the finish.

Since the cabinet hangs on the wall a door latch is necessary. The most convenient latch is the magnetic kind, and since the doors come together at the center with no center post in the way, one magnetic latch set in the center will catch the top inside corner of both doors. The metal which comes with the latch is quite soft and can be shaped with tin snips to fit the edge of the doors.

Illus. 120. The shelves can be rearranged to suit other uses.

Illus. 121. Exploded view of the spice cabinet.

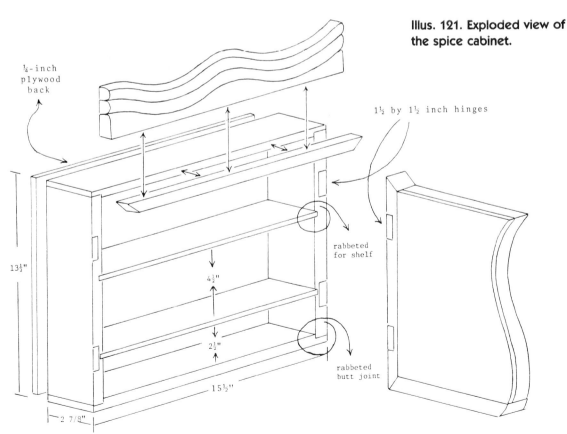

¼-inch plywood back

1½ by 1½ inch hinges

rabbeted for shelf

rabbeted butt joint

13½"

4½"

2½"

15½"

2 7/8"

Test Tube Bud Vase

Illus. 122. The three-curve bud vase.

It is sometimes fun to start a project with only a vague notion of what the end result will be and how to get to it, especially when the project is not very big and doesn't call for a lot of expensive wood. Such is the case with the test tube bud vase. There was an 8-inch length of 4 × 4 fir lying

on the workbench, so I decided to try to saw a spiral which would wind around a test tube and function as a bud vase. The results are not quite spirals, but the effect is perhaps more interesting than if they were.

There are only two patterns here, but variations can go on forever (Illus. 123). Visualizing the end results of a three-dimensional object when it has no parallel planes is extremely difficult, but as long as the lines on a given side do not cross you will not end up with two separate pieces, each with a hole in its middle. Most of my fascination with this project is that the results remain hidden until the final saw cut.

The first step is to find the center of the 4 × 4 and drill a hole for the test tube. The test tube I used was 6 inches long and ¾ inch in diameter with a ⅞-inch flange at the top, so I drilled a 13/64-wide hole to allow the tube to settle into the wood a little. There is no standard test tube size, so if you want to use a different-size tube, make sure you change the dimensions accordingly.

Try out the test tube to make sure it will slide to the bottom of the hole without binding; then lay out the pattern (Illus. 125a–125b) on two sides of the block, at 90° to each other. Saw out one side first and keep the cut-off parts, so they can be used to hold the piece while the second side is being sawn (Illus. 125c).

With both sides sawn out the only thing left to do is the sanding. A 3½ × ¾-inch drum sander is ideal. The arrangement shown in Illus. 124 works well and is inexpensive. The ¾-inch-dowel has a ¼-inch rod in one end for chucking up in the drill. Drill a hole through the dowel and the rod and use an old worn-out drill bit to pin the two together. Glue a ½-inch dowel to the other end of the ¾-inch dowel, and slip the ½-inch dowel into a bearing from an old lawn-mower wheel. Glue a piece of sandpaper onto the dowel. This gives a firm, but not hard, backing for better sanding.

Since it's likely the vase will have water dripped on it from time to time, varnish is an appropriate finish.

Illus. 123. The four-curve bud vase.

Illus. 124. The homemade drum sander is good for sanding the in's and out's of the test tube bud vase.

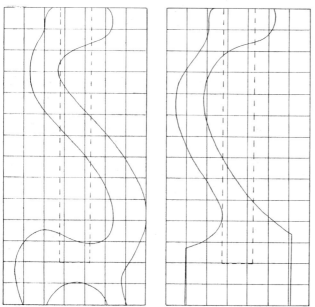

Illus. 125a. This is the simpler of the two designs. It requires a 7-inch length of 4 by 4. Enlarge to ½-inch squares.

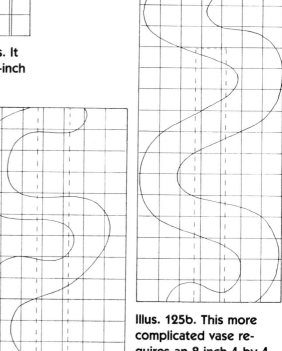

Illus. 125b. This more complicated vase requires an 8-inch 4 by 4. Enlarge to ½-inch squares.

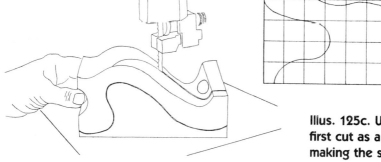

Illus. 125c. Using the sawn off part from the first cut as a holder for work piece while making the second cut.

Bentwood Mirror Frame

It would certainly be an omission on my part if, after all my talk about resawing, I didn't include a project which used it, in this case a bentwood project.

I love bending wood. It always gives me the impression of complete mastery over the material, although usually somewhere in the middle of the project it seems to be the other way around. In the end, though, I always come out with the upper hand. The secret is control of both the wood and yourself.

When bending wood you'll need a form. The form acts as something of a mould for your shape. The form should always be thicker than the wood itself so that you can bend the wood around it and come out with the shape you want. More on this to come.

There are three methods of preparing wood for bending: steaming, soaking, and cold. We'll use soaking for this project, for the simple reason that it's an easy method of preparing the wood. No steam box is required, no fire, just a container to hold the water. I used the bathtub. Fill it up only a few inches and add a little dishwashing liquid or fabric softener to the water, but be sure to rinse this off before clamping.

The frame is five strips of oak (red or white will do), 36 inches long, 1 inch wide and resawn to ³⁄₁₆ inch thick. Rip the inside strip to ³⁄₈ inch

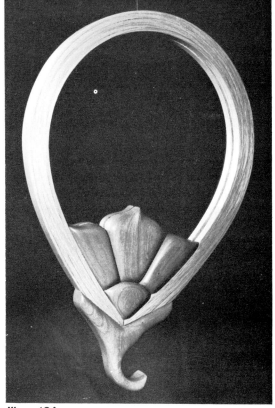

Illus. 126.

wide so you can lay it into the form first for the mirror brace (the part that will hold the glass). Saw the strips and lightly sand them to remove saw marks. Soak them overnight in a few inches of water, weighted down with a rock or bottle of shampoo.

While the strips are soaking, make the form, which is the shape you're bending the wood to. You'll need 3 pieces of ½-inch plywood, one for the base and two for the actual shape. Make sure the base is large enough to

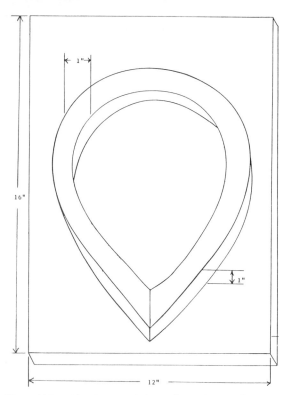

Illus. 127a. The base of the mirror frame form is ½-inch plywood, laid out as shown.

be clamped to a bench without being in the way of the clamps that will hold the strips to the form. Take the other two pieces and cut them to shape (Illus. 127a). Glue these pieces together, clean up the edges on the belt sander and cut out the center of the form to allow a better surface for the clamps. Screw some scrap 1 by across the saw kerf on the bottom of the form. This will keep the kerf from closing up when the strips are bent around the form. Wax the form thoroughly before gluing up, otherwise your mirror frame will be forever glued to the form (Illus. 128).

Now bend the strips around the form while still wet, and hold them with a web clamp or belt clamp until they dry. After the strips are dry, there will be some springback but they will be much easier to handle.

I glued my frame up in two sessions for two reasons. First, the two inner strips will need to be trimmed—either clamp them into position on the form and saw them on the band saw or by hand, or mark them on the form, take them off and saw and reclamp them. So, getting them positioned for gluing is a little bit tricky. The other reason is that trying to glue all five strips at once, bend them into position, and clamp them is a hard job for more hands than the normal person possesses. The last three strips are much easier; they don't have to be joined and so are much easier to position. Make sure, though, that you keep the first two strips on the form when doing the next three, or they all won't fit.

The glue used in laminated wood bending must be of a different ilk than the wood glues we have come to know and love. Titebond and Elmer's Carpenter's Glue (polyvinyl resin emulsions) have a problem called cold creep (page 32), which, over time, will cause any bentwood project to completely unravel. You should use either epoxy (not the five-minute kind) or Weldwood Plastic resin. Neither of these glues is as convenient to work with as PVA's, but they won't allow cold creep.

The frame should be face down on the form so that you'll have a flush surface on the face side of the frame. Wipe out any excess glue which squeezes out between the mirror

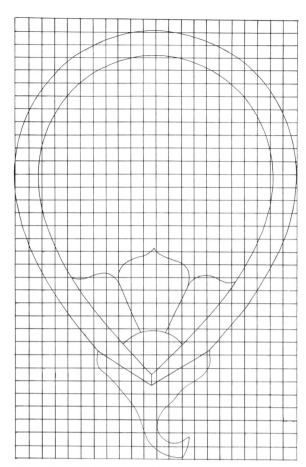

Illus. 127b. Enlarge to ½-inch squares. Make the form the size of the inner oval.

brace strip and the second strip, so as not to foil the mirror brace.

The flower is 1½-inch-thick cherry and made like band saw art (page 96). Transfer the pattern to the wood with carbon paper and saw out the individual pieces. Rabbet the back of the flower petals to match the mirror brace in a straight line across the bottom. When you cut the flower stem, use it to mark the lower frame to insure a good cut and fit.

After the flower is sanded and stained with a little mahogany stain to increase the contrast, glue it into place; the stem first, then the center of the flower, then the outside petals, and finally the center petal.

Finish the frame with spray varnish and rub it with linseed oil and 0000 steel wool.

To make sure I would get a good fit on the mirror I made a poster-board pattern of the mirror and took it to the glass shop to have the mirror cut. I got a good fit.

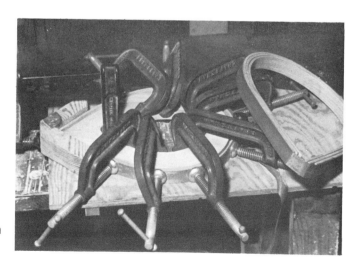

Illus. 128. Lay up the oak on the form in two gluing sessions. The last three strips remain held in place with a web clamp.

117

Bentwood Wind Chime

I couldn't stop at just one bentwood project. This one uses a different type of form, and shows how much rigidity can be achieved by bending and laminating two pieces of wood. The strips of wood involved here are much shorter and a little easier to handle than the mirror frame. The main support is 18 inches long and the branch and suspended branch are both 14 inches. All the pieces are 3/16 inch thick, as in the mirror, but only 3/8-wide white oak. A strip of cherry veneer lies in between.

Soak both the oak and the cherry overnight to make them easier to

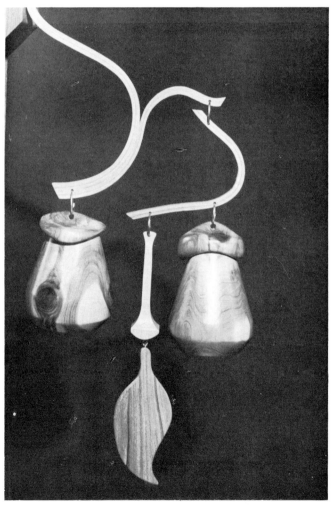

Illus. 129.

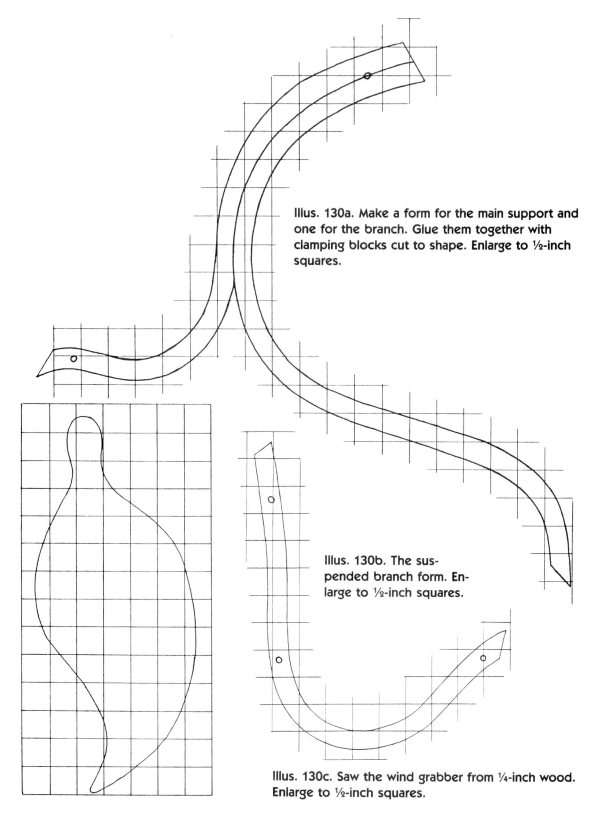

Illus. 130a. Make a form for the main support and one for the branch. Glue them together with clamping blocks cut to shape. Enlarge to ½-inch squares.

Illus. 130b. The suspended branch form. Enlarge to ½-inch squares.

Illus. 130c. Saw the wind grabber from ¼-inch wood. Enlarge to ½-inch squares.

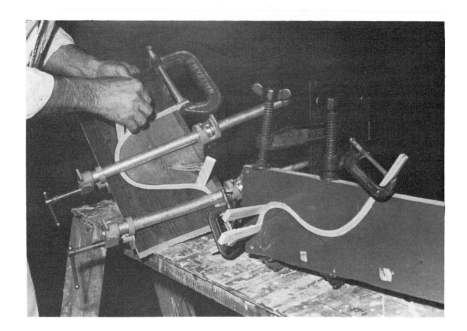

Illus. 131. Clamp the forms together, with wedges to fill the empty spots.

bend. These bends will get very close to the maximum curve, so it's very helpful to take each piece of wood and bow it a little to get the bend started before you clamp it into the form for drying. This prebending helps the wood start stretching on the outside of the curve and compressing on the inside, sort of like an athlete warming up.

The forms are simply pieces of 1-inch-wide scrap with the shapes sawn out lengthwise (Illus. 130a–130b). Clamp the wood between the two pieces and let it dry (Illus. 131). Use the same form for giving the oak and cherry together. You'll need three forms, one for the main support, one for the branch, and one for the suspended branch. Be sure to use a plastic resin or epoxy glue. Since all the ends of the bentwood part hang free, cold creep (from using a PVA) will distort the shape.

The bells are cedar, 5½ inches long and 4 inches in diameter (Illus. 132b). The exact shape of the bells is not critical as long as the clapper can strike them.

First saw off the top along the curved line. Using a compass, lay out the diameter of the inner and outer walls on top of the bell. Saw out the inside space and glue the kerf shut. (It's much easier to do this before sawing the outside shape. Mark the bevel heights in the outside of the bell with your scriber and saw the upper bevel (page 25) first.

The tops of the bells require two saw cuts, 90° from each other. The part that is removed is where the wire link will be inserted. Hold the part removed by the first cut in place while you make the second cut. Accuracy is not critical, since the two should not look exactly alike. Now saw the tops to about 3 inches in diameter. The remaining shaping of the tops, rounding the edges and smoothing out the top, is done on the belt sander. When sanding, remember the tops should have an organic appearance rather than a machined one. After all the shaping and sanding is done, glue the bells and tops together with five-minute epoxy.

The clapper is a simple hammer shape made of 1-inch wide oak and attached to the wind grabber with small screw eyes (Illus. 132a). The wind grabber is flat ¼-inch hardwood or plywood (Illus. 130c).

When all the parts are finished assemble the chime with loops of 18-gauge house wiring stripped of insulation and rolled around a piece of 1-inch-diameter dowel. Drill ⅛-inch holes for the wire in the appropriate places.

Illus. 132a. The clapper is oak and hangs just long enough to strike the fat part of the bells.

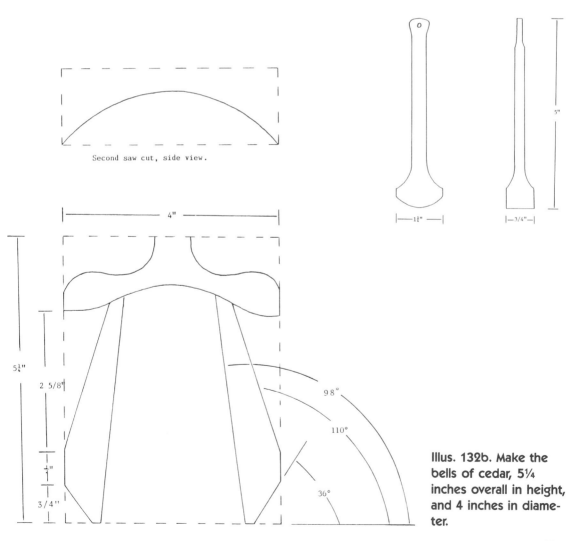

Second saw cut, side view.

4"

5¼"

2 5/8"

⅛"

3/4"

98°

110°

36°

1¼"

3/4"

5"

Illus. 132b. Make the bells of cedar, 5¼ inches overall in height, and 4 inches in diameter.

Appendix

THE PANTOGRAPH

Illus. 133. The pantograph in action.

A pantograph is based on four-bar parallel linkage geometry. The four sticks are of equal length (it doesn't matter what length as long as they cross each other in the middle), although the longer the sticks you use, the larger the drawing you can make. A 24-inch pantograph, like the one shown in Illus. 134, is a pretty good size. The sticks are 24½ × ¾ × ¼-inch hardwood. Mark the center of each stick and drill 6 holes, ³⁄₁₆ inch in diameter, 1 inch apart on either side of the center line. (The center of each stick should be marked permanently, so it will be easy to find without hav-

ing to count holes.) Drill another ³⁄₁₆-inch-diameter hole ⅜ inch from the end of each stick except where the pencil and the tracer points will be. These holes should be ¼ inch in diameter, which will fit most 6-sided pencils quite snugly.

Use ¼-inch-diameter dowel for the tracer point so you can switch it with the pencil when reducing. Sharpen the dowel to about the point you would find on a dull pencil. Make sure the tracer is smooth, or you'll tear the paper when you move the point over it.

Use ¾ by 8-32 bolts at the other

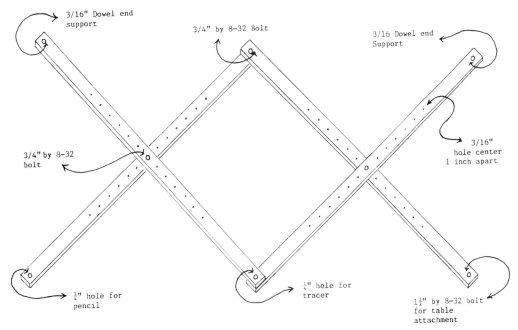

Illus. 134. The pantograph is four 24½-inch long sticks arranged as shown.

attachment points. They will thread themselves into the ³⁄₁₆-inch-diameter holes and hold snugly without nuts. Use a 1½-inch 8-32 bolt to attach the end to the table. Embed the nut with glue, into a $2 \times 4 \times ¼$-inch piece of white pine, which can be clamped to a table without scratching the table top. Support the two free ends of the pantograph with ³⁄₁₆-inch dowel, slightly rounded on one end.

Set the pantograph at the center crossings to get used to the machine. At this setting, a ½ inch line will come out to 1 inch. Extend the left crossing points out to the ends or to the last holes and the images will be the same size. Extend the right crossing points to the last holes and ½ inch will equal 1¾ inches. Combinations of one crossing moved out and the other moved in will give an almost

infinite variation in scale. The pantograph will take some getting use to, but it is one of the most accurate and speedy ways to scale up a drawing.

THE OVALER

Projects like the oval flame, the nut bowl and even the band saw art need ovals. Drawing ovals is hard, takes a lot of time and measuring, and never comes out quite right. So, here's an ovaler. This tool will draw ovals in three different sizes and many different measurements. Making it won't take long and can save you time, even if you only draw three ovals in your lifetime.

The smallest oval the ovaler will draw is 5½ inches long by 3⅞ inches wide. If you need a smaller oval the copy machine will do a better job. It is almost impossible to make a smaller ovaler.

Begin with a 3 × 3 × ¾-inch block of hardwood (Illus. 135). On two edges of the block draw a line ⅜ inch from the top. Mark the center of the block on this line. Drill a ⁵⁄₁₆-inch-diameter hole all the way through with a drill press or dowelling jig.

Draw two lines across the face of the block, each ³⁄₁₆ inch wide, which when sawn into will open the center of the ⁵⁄₁₆-inch holes. Now saw off the corners of the block, leaving ⅛ inch of wood beside the holes. This will let you draw smaller ovals. Sand the holes and edges for easier sliding and then wax the block with a hard wax.

The travellers (which allow the arm to pivot) are ⁵⁄₁₆-inch dowel, each ⅞-inch long. Sand them down so they slide easily in the track. This is best done before you cut the short pieces to length. Then drill a ⅛-inch-diameter hole in the center of the ⅞-inch lengths of dowel. Now you can saw them to length. Then give a ⁵⁄₁₆-inch length of ⅛-inch dowel into the ⁵⁄₁₆ by ⅞-inch dowel and wax both pieces.

The arm on which the pencil rides can be as long as you like, and sliding the pencil in and out will enlarge the oval. The three small holes (centered ⅜ inch apart) change the length to width ratio. Center the hole at the end of the arm ⅞ inch from the nearest ratio hole. The arm on my ovaler is 4½ × ⅝ × ⅛ inches, so the largest oval it will draw is 9¼ inches in length.

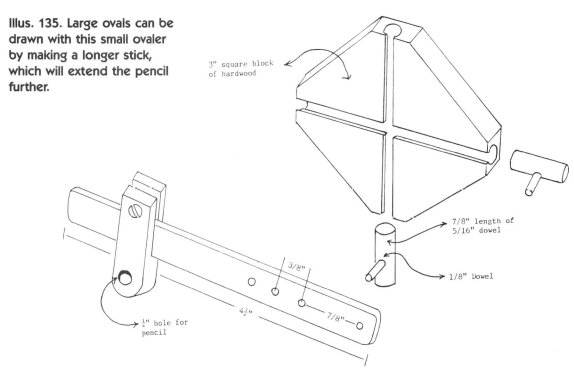

Illus. 135. Large ovals can be drawn with this small ovaler by making a longer stick, which will extend the pencil further.

3" square block of hardwood

7/8" length of 5/16" dowel

1/8" Dowel

3/8"

4½"

7/8"

¼" hole for pencil

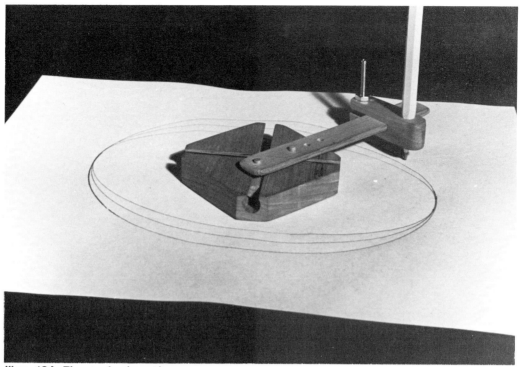

Illus. 136. The ovaler in action.

USING A SCRIBER

Illus. 137. The scriber squaring a log.

A scriber allows you to draw a straight line around a cylinder (Illus. 137). It's almost indispensable for some of the projects in this book, especially when you want a cylinder's sides absolutely 90° from its bottom. This must be done before you can stand a log on its end and saw it to shape with accuracy.

To use it, first, saw off the section of log needed as squarely as possible at one end. Stand the log up on the workbench and, if its sides are fairly parallel, square it from the table,

Illus. 138. The scriber can also draw lines for lids.

holding it in position with wedges. Now the scriber can slide around the log on the bench top and give you a line to saw which is square to the sides of the log. You can set the height of the scriber's pencil to the lowest point on the log to remove the least amount of wood (Illus. 138).

If the log's sides are not parallel enough to let you square from the bench top, you might want to saw the log into a cylinder with the end only eyeballed square; then start the squaring procedure.

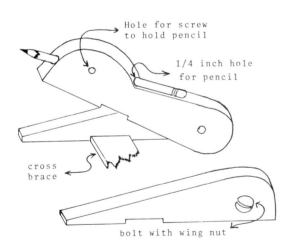

Hole for screw to hold pencil

1/4 inch hole for pencil

cross brace

bolt with wing nut

Illus. 139a (above) and Illus. 139b (right). The scriber is 5 inches long, made of hardwood. Enlarge the pattern to ½-inch squares.

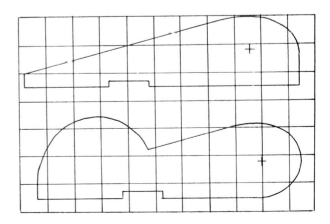

INDEX